FREE ADVICE

FREE ADVICE

Uncommon Wisdom from a Marketing Muse

LAURI LEVY

Open Door Publications

Free Advice
Uncommon Wisdom from a Marketing Muse
is a work of nonfiction
by Lauri Levy

Published by
Open Door Publications
Yardley, PA 19067
www.OpenDoorPublications.com

All interior photos by Lauri Levy, from the Levy family collection or provided by GL&S, Inc.

ISBN: 978-0-9981208-6-7

Printed in the United States

First Edition

Cover design by Eric Labacz

To my Jeanne, my partner in everything.

To my parents, Eva and Ivor Levy, and to my grandparents, Maurice D. and Minnie Berg, who gave me all the basics to succeed and all the encouragement I needed to follow my dreams.

“Seriously, I have been talking to people about you and they said you were the first person to buy my show—way back when we were first starting out. And you didn’t wait for the ratings to come in and you didn’t wait to see what other people thought. And it’s nice that you came on at the start. I’m really grateful to you because it’s a rough business and very few people say, ‘yeah, I believe’ and you obviously said that and I thank you very much.”

Joan Rivers
Portland, Oregon 1991

Table of Contents

INTRODUCTION

Throughout my career, I have been often asked, "Just a quick question, how did you get in the business?"

As far back as I have been able to track, my ancestors came from Eastern Europe, migrating first to England, and then my parents and grandparents came to the States. But no matter where they were born, they were born to sell. It is in the genes. We all got the same abilities. It's cultural—we have the gift of gab, and we can read faces.

My grandfather was a salesman through and through. He was written up in a variety of periodicals lauding his skills, and was always tops in my book. I would watch him in action when I was old enough to know there was action going on. My grandmother and I would visit him at the store where he worked selling men's clothing when we were on a shopping junket downtown. He sold many things in his long career, but he ended his career selling suits, and he was well-known for it. There he would be with his boutonniere on his lapel—always a miniature rose from his garden—always looking the part. He was always dressed for success, but was very humble in his approach, considering his accomplishments in his craft. My grandfather was extremely happy to be a big fish in a very small pond because he had other priorities in life—his family. He always balanced his life perfectly. I learned from my grandfather how to be successful and still not lose sight of the bigger prize, which, in turn, helps your career.

My grandmother never worked an honest day in her life, as my dad used to say lovingly. While researching my family tree I noticed "cap maker" listed as her occupation on her wedding certificate, and I found that interesting. For the record, she never claimed to be a cap maker but her people were cap makers from way back, so I guess that qualified for her to be one, too. No matter, because my grandma taught me the value of quality over quantity and why buying the best is always the way to go. If you have to wait to buy the best, then wait until you can. This was an invaluable lesson that has shaped my life in both business and personal matters. Surround yourself with the best, and you never go wrong. This lesson I learned directly from my grandmother.

My mother, their daughter, was a chip off the old block. Like her father, my mom also spent her career in sales—in retail—and was always *numero uno* no matter where or for whom she worked. She was a major fashion dog from the word go, and always had the courage of her convictions when it came to the latest looks and trends. She always told me that I had to "look the part." She was never a follower, and this spirit of leadership and guts was something I got from my mom. She was very successful in sales, and she ran circles around everyone, often women half her age, usually selling more working part time than those around her did working 40 hours a week. My mom always won sales contests, and the culmination of her accomplishments was when she was awarded the "Secret Shopper of the Year" designation at the major upscale, super-regional mall where she worked. Out of all the employees at all the stores in this mall, routinely recognized as one of the top in per square foot sales in the country, my mother took the top prize for customer service. No surprise, it was totally deserved.

My father was also a natural talent in many ways. He was always running for most popular in whatever crowd he was in, and yet, he had a very quiet ego. My dad was one of the smartest and genuinely nicest people I have ever known, and he never acted as if he thought so. He came to work in sales late in his career after quitting a company that he had been with for 27 years—ever since he came to America. He worked in marketing, too, and as I remember the story went that the company he worked for was firing senior executives right before their retirement. It seemed as if they did this to reduce payout of their earned compensation. They did this to my dad's boss, whom he admired, and my father found this behavior to be so unethical that he quit on principle. I remember being shocked when I heard this because my dad would not quit his job willy-nilly, so I knew it must have been something big for him to do so. This was a teachable moment because through his example and leadership, I learned that ethics have tremendous value.

Naturally, things worked out well for him after that because he took a job in sales. He said it was fun and easy, because for him it was; he had all the natural traits required to be successful at it. This was at a large retail company with many locations and hundreds of employees. My dad was number one in sales each of the 15 years he worked there. My parents' den walls were covered with his awards. As I said, he was a natural. He had no formal training; he just had "it." People give money to people they like and my dad was proof positive of that theory.

So that's how I got into it.

From our history, each of us has a combination of natural traits. That means that the best way to be successful is to focus on those things we naturally do best. Unfortunately, some people possess very little of what is necessary to excel at any number of things they insist on doing. A lack of natural talent does not stop them from thinking they can do things that they cannot do well. This is especially prevalent in the marketing arena.

Hello, USA 1948

This was the catalyst for writing this book. I want to shed light on what it really takes to be successful as a marketer. So sit back and enjoy my real-life fables, and please take full advantage of my "free advice."

Lauri Levy

Part One
BACKGROUND

1

FOUNDATION ESSENTIALS

Inclination

My story begins at age 12 when a very significant opportunity was presented to me, one that would be the catalyst for the rest of my life. It was the summer of 1964, and a cousin of ours sent a plane ticket to me so I could come and spend the summer with her. Yetta lived in New York City, and she said she would show me everything there was to see…and she did.

At the time, she was a widow in her 60s and a real pistol, our family's very own "Auntie Mame." She lived on the upper west side of Manhattan, and she was totally enthralling to me from the moment we met. She was exotic and worldly and extremely interesting. She was fun and entertaining with a special sizzle all her own. We played canasta in her small kitchen in between the field trips, and talked for hours. She took me everywhere—to the Metropolitan Museum where she was on the board, to a United Nations Security Council meeting, to the World's Fair, plus a few side excursions including a dude ranch in nearby Pennsylvania.

New York was totally and completely for me, and it was love at first sight. I felt at home there because I was in my element. New York City is the center of the advertising world, a retail mecca and sociological study the likes of which cannot be matched. New York City is the center of the art world, too, a compelling mix of cultures, and definitely high energy. I was a duck in water. Throughout my life I was always asked if I was from New York, which I always took as a compliment despite being very proud of where I was raised, in Portland, Oregon. Even at a young age, I could see this was going to be a preview of coming attractions for me, and, in fact, it came to pass that New York City would become an important backdrop for a big part of my life.

My career began shortly thereafter. I had stints in babysitting of course, and selling Camp Fire mints. Babysitting provided an allowance, and Camp Fire provided a lot of earned business beads, but then I got my first real job. During my last two years of high school, afternoons were spent at a printing company working for a professional friend of my dad, one of his suppliers. I earned high school credits for working, in addition to the pay, so the hours I put in paid double. Here I learned to set type, do print layouts for corporate magazines and direct mail, and I learned a variety of production skills that I still use today. Back in the Stone Age, everything was manual. There was no computer anything. Type was set with a machine, and then the work was printed onto paper and pasted up on boards that were then put onto a press. I got involved in the whole process up close and personal. I knew the printing business, per se, was not something I would continue to do, but it gave me a taste of creating something and seeing it come to life. I liked that part of the business and still do.

I applied the creative process I had learned in the printing business to help launch my first company in the summer before my senior year in high school. It all came about because I decided to make myself a suede belt. I don't know where I got the idea that I could make one; perhaps it was because I came from cap makers—a family trait coming home to roost. Perhaps it was a natural evolution from my dad who had a job as a pattern maker when he was a teenager working in the fashion factories in Manchester, England, before he went into the Royal Air Force, married my mom, and came to the USA.

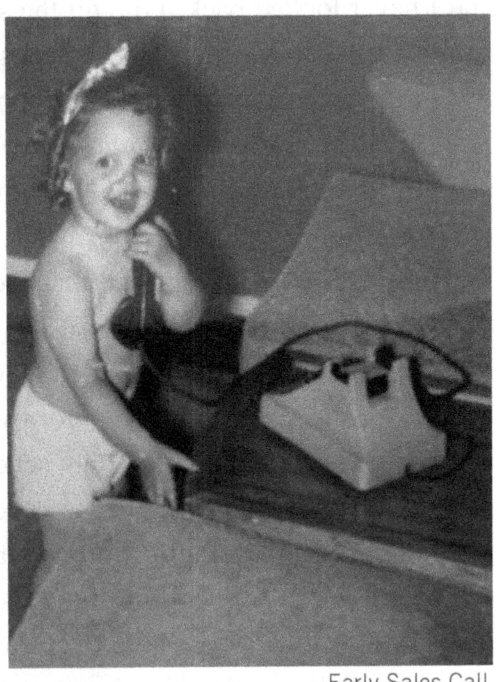
Early Sales Call

Regardless of the propeller, I wanted a belt I had seen in my mind, inspired by the fashion magazines and my fashion-forward mother's influence, and I proceeded to create it. The next thing I knew, I was taking orders. I sold them in my high school bookstore and also in a couple of other schools where I had connections. I created my first brand, called "Inclination," and my dad helped me create hangtags and invoices.

The belts gained popularity, and so I brought in two partners. Pelts of suede and leather materialized into money, and I never looked back. I did all the selling and sold the belts from samples to a variety of the best stores in town, including two of the biggest names in the fashion retail world to this day.

However, it was a very clever buyer for a well-known and beloved local junior women's fashion chain who placed an order that took Inclination up a notch. I still remember the feeling I had when Judi placed that order for 14 dozen belts. I thought I'd hit the big time.

Inclination was doing well and was providing as I had hoped. We made enough money for two of us to go to Europe, as we had planned to do after high school graduation. My third partner used her share of the proceeds to help with college moving expenses. Going to Europe was one of my very early short-term goals. The bottom line was I needed enough profit to last me as long as possible overseas. That turned out to be two and a half months, based on my desired level of comfort and access to good food. No youth hostels or hitchhiking for me, even back then.

So there was a finite timeline to this venture. I knew I couldn't sustain my business because two thirds of the partners were heading off to Europe and the other third to college. Immediately before our planned departures, we got a large reorder. I hadn't planned on this happening because I was so focused on my trip and delivering what we had already promised. I never thought about them calling us for more, since prior to this, it was always the other way around—me calling them to check on sales and to see if they needed more. I had no choice but to confess to my best customer that the business was closing and there would be no more deliveries. It was time to move on. The world was waiting.

No belt was going to tie me down. It was only a coincidence that this fashion chain shuttered its stores several years later. I am certain this had nothing to do with my belts, and Judi, the buyer, ended up with a very successful career, a giant in the retailing world, and we would remain friends over the years.

The two and a half months I spent in Europe were a real motivator, and because of them, I adopted the motto I saw in an ad for *Travel and Leisure* magazine:

"Travel is not a reward for working, but homework for living."

I completely subscribe to that statement.

Going to college was always something I planned to do when I got back from Europe, but that two-and-a-half-month sojourn got in the way of my plans. The experience altered my thinking big time, and the detour is still paying dividends. Of course, I came from people who emigrated from one country to another so it's no wonder that I love to travel, but when I first went to Europe I had no idea how it would totally change my life.

I was still ready to give traditional learning another shot, but after two terms at a local state university I learned that I would have to take matters into my own hands. This college experience was a major disappointment to me. The classes were not inspirational or motivational, not even the History of Art class.

Here I was, just back from two and a half months walking in the steps of history and art in Europe and now I felt like I was watching someone else's photos from their trip to Europe. This was definitely not working for me. Once you see London, Paris, and Florence, it's too hard to sit still in a classroom looking at pictures projected onto a blank wall. Gothic architecture looks so much better from across the piazza sitting in a well-placed, picturesque outdoor café with a latte and a croissant.

I wanted to enroll in a Graphic Design class, but that was not possible. The Basic Design class I was forced to take first was the final blow. Having been recognized for artistic capability starting in elementary school, where I won a school-wide poster design contest in third grade, in addition to being selected to be in a special art class from first through sixth grade, did not spare me from the punishment of making color wheels for the umpteenth time in this mandatory prerequisite. For the record, I was also the least talented artist in that class, so the suffering was felt all around. Was this higher education?

My short stay in college soured me on the university experience until 30 years later when I returned to higher ed to take a photography class at Parsons, part of the New School University in Manhattan. Now, that was more like it—no pre-requisites required, just a good eye, great subject matter, and the ability to capture it was all that was needed. That first class with Harvey, a well-known New York City photographer and author, encouraged me to take other photography classes including those at ICP, and that led me to enter many juried shows.

I won awards for my work in art shows on both coasts and was especially proud to win one at The Salmagundi Club, New York's prestigious art institution.

I showed my photographs for many years in gallery shows in New York City and Los Angeles. It is always a thrill to be able to share my experiences traveling the world through my photographs, something I still love to do to this day.

Back in those old days at the state university, I was forced into a system that was not a good fit for me, did not keep my attention, and did not stimulate my curiosity. I knew sitting there was not going to pay my freight back to Europe where I longed to go.

When I left that university in my late teens, I had 44 credit hours. I had completed two terms, plus I had a few credits earned from two classes, Italian and Basic Composition, that I took during my senior year of high school so I could get the student credentials I needed in order to save a few bucks in Europe with discounts on trains and museum tickets. I spent most of my time in the cafeteria playing cards. The credit hours and card sense were not the only things I got out of college though, because in the end I learned a lot. I realized that I did not like going to college to relearn what I already knew or to attempt to learn something that could be better learned somewhere else. It was not what I had expected and at that time it seemed far less, educationally speaking, as compared to my really great high school experience.

It was time to move on and get back to my life as an entrepreneurial businesswoman. I thought I had enough credentials, and nothing was going to stop me. Inclination was only the first taste of business success for me, but one that I savored and wanted to repeat. It was just simply about selling something I created, knowing I had to do it, believing that it was right, and trusting in my abilities.

Many years later, after founding my advertising agency, I had another encounter with higher education based on a recommendation. I still had a regret about not getting a degree, so it was suggested that I seek credits for lifetime learning at another local college. After a few interviews, and after submitting a written biography, they asked me why at this point in my life I was interested in a Bachelor's degree. I told them I really wanted a Master's degree because I thought it would be helpful in marketing a book I was in the process of developing, planning to complete, and to publish one day. I was then accepted into the Master's program in Business Management based on my real-world experience.

In the end, I chose not to enroll because once I saw how much it was going to cost me for these credentials, I decided that the 44 credit hours were enough after all.

As you can see, I didn't need a degree to write or get my book published.

2

MAXIMIZING OPPORTUNITY

May I Help You?

After my quick university stopover, I took my abilities out on the street and went looking for a job. The first stop was the department store where my grandfather worked. I walked right in, up to personnel, and said, "I am looking for work, and I want a creative job, nothing boring, I don't want to be a cashier or work as a saleswoman." Even then I knew that if you don't decide what you are worth, who will?

The nice lady to whom I was speaking replied in a whisper as if she were a librarian, "Sorry but we have no openings to offer you right now, perhaps you can check back with us again." I guess she was trying to be kind.

Well, not surprised or unshaken, I promptly marched across the street to their competitor, the other and much larger department store in town. Both stores had their special touches that the community knew and loved. This was home to Santa and the annual and official holiday parade as compared with the Cinnamon Bear across the street.

I went up to their personnel department, the second performance of the day, and gave my same list of demands. The woman in the cubicle across the desk from me spoke louder, which was good since she was saying something I wanted to hear. "Take a seat out front and I'll be back to you."

Apparently she called down to the fashion office—a store department I did not know existed—to speak with the fashion director. She said she "had someone who she thought would be an asset to the company but did not know any place other than there that would be a fit."

This was on Monday afternoon and I started as the fashion office manager, assisting the director, two days later and stayed with the company for three and a half years.

Life in the fashion office was always interesting, made to order actually. A constant swarm of models, portfolios, runways, buyers, merchandise managers, advertising people and the folks in the display department swirling about like a merry-go-round of creative energy. I thrived in the stimulating environment full of many smart women including a boss who later became my second and long-term business partner.

I met both of my ad agency partners while I worked in the fashion office. My first partner, Deidre, came to our office because she was on the *Mademoiselle* magazine college board, which was basically an unpaid focus group for the magazine and additional free workforce for us. The store would hold events co-sponsored by *Mademoiselle*, and all members of their college board within close range would be called into action to assist in their promotional activities. These young women were a great ball of energy and help.

The same strategy was utilized when the store created its own Career Board consisting of a few dozen key women leaders in the community. They would come into the store once a month for a free lunch in exchange for feedback on all fashion marketing subjects. I made a note to self: Food is bait to gain free marketing advice.

There was usually some major event being developed and executed by the fashion office, such as traveling bridal shows to all the stores in the chain and regular presentations of the latest trends to the store's fashion buyers and assistant buyers. The fashion office also created the store's fashion calendar of events, and we worked hand in hand with the company's display department to help present a consistent fashion message via the mannequins throughout the store and in the store's famous windows.

It was a fantastic experience for so many reasons, and I often thought it would make a great sitcom with all the personalities and their wheelings and dealings. As it turned out, I had no idea at the time that a retail sitcom was in my future.

This was definitely one of my college educations, done in the office instead of the classroom. It was the best groundwork I could have imagined to prepare me for owning an ad agency because of the systems management I learned at the store. For every aspect of every project there was a system, and for every activity there was a chain of command. For the most part, it worked beautifully, and I carried those practical lessons throughout my career and use them to this day. I am very organized thanks to the responsibility sheet approach I learned on this job.

Organization is a skill that is essential to being on the top of any game.

I worked long hours, sometimes seven days a week, and never minded the majority of it because it was fun and engaging. Much like life itself, time flies when you are happy at work.

However, there were occasional times when the work was not so stimulating, supporting my initial reluctance to work on the retail floor. These were times when the "non-selling" department personnel were called into action to help with other store activities that required all hands on deck. For example, twice a year in January and June we would be farmed out to assist with inventory, and I would end up in a variety of departments, from linens to boys clothing, to help count the merchandise. This was definitely not the fun part. One time I was inadvertently spared because I was left off the reassignment list. I was told that this was a fluke, not likely to ever happen again, and I should enjoy it.

The holiday season was not a jolly time to be in the fashion office for me either. Since everything we did stopped for the most important selling season of the year, once again all the non-selling staff were given special holiday assignments between Thanksgiving and Christmas. This would be a post in gift wrap or helping in Santa's Holiday Lane. One year I ended up at the "May I Help You" desk. I am positive this was payback for having escaped doing inventory once before.

The "May I Help You" setup consisted of a booth on the main floor, situated under the store's famous giant clock. Under the clock was a well-established meeting spot where shoppers would reconvene after completing their individual missions. The booth was small and cramped, barely big enough for a stool with a backrest, and I was stuck in there for too many hours at a time. It was torture. Shoppers would come by and ask for directions or to buy a gift certificate, which at least broke the boredom. Occasionally shoppers would use me as an ear for their complaints.

I knew I had to do something to get out of that booth as soon as possible. So a holiday miracle of an idea was hatched when I suddenly claimed to have developed a serious enough back condition that would keep me out of duty for almost the entire two-week "May I Help You" run. I am not proud of that move, but I did come back one day before it was supposed to be over to show that I still had a wee bit of that company can-do spirit.

This experience taught me that I was not a good fit for this type of customer service.

We had a lot of fun coming up with ways to bring in the

right customers to the store. We did all kinds of events and fashion shows and one of the best was served up with a happy hour billed as "Fifty Cent Highballs and Cheap Champagne" in an after-work special event. We packed them in, and once again it demonstrated the power of food and drink to draw a crowd. I used this gold mine tactic in different ways for a variety of clients over the years and it worked like a charm every time.

During my three-and-a-half-year stint in the fashion office I also met many helpful contacts, some of which became clients later on. In addition to both of my business partners, one of the best people I met turned out to be a future employer.

It was inevitable that in order to move up I had to move on. The times were changing, and the prevailing winds had me heading out. The fashion office was evolving. I had done a great job organizing the office and assisting in a variety of ways to include creative copywriting assignments. Naturally, I thought the advertising department was going to be a natural next stop for me, so I went up to personnel to see what could be done to transfer me there.

The outcome was surprising. They said I was an asset, knew I had talent, and they did not want to lose me but…there were no openings in the advertising department at the moment. Personnel did a stellar job trying to convince me to stay with the company and go through their executive training program that would lead me into a career in merchandising, in other words, a buyer. I knew this was not in my game plan and we parted ways.

When I left the store I told myself that if I did business with them again it would be on my terms. I had no idea how quickly that opportunity would come to pass.

No sooner had I left the store when I got a call from the advertising department wanting to hire me as a freelance writer for a White Sale catalog. Of course, I said yes and gave them my price for the job that was equal to two months of pay at the rate I was making when I left. They hired me, and I was so happy until I realized that this work was not my cup of tea after all. It was tedious, boring subject matter, and very unfulfilling. I promised myself that I would never do that again.

Fortunately, I did not end up in that store's advertising department, and I will always be grateful that the winds of fate blew me in another direction: to go out on my own.

Always seize opportunity when it presents itself because experience helps in decision making, and all things happen for a reason.

3

SELLING 101

I'll Never Call You Again, Sign Here

I remember returning to New York in the winter of 1978. I am certain I have lived in New York City in a previous lifetime, and I was feeling this now quite intensely. Thanks to my cousin Yetta years before, my love affair with this city started early in my life.

Fast forward 15 years or so when I was in Manhattan on vacation, traveling with my friend, former boss, and soon-to-be second business partner. Susan was there in her official capacity as corporate fashion merchandising director to see the fall presentations at two of the largest and most influential fashion magazines, among other meetings and duties. I was there to shop, go to museums, eat, and have fun.

During that trip, there was a major winter storm of epic proportions, even for the East Coast, that left 14 inches of snow on the ground and brought the city to a standstill for a day. I remember thinking how amazing it was that even Macy's and Bloomingdale's closed. That was a rare occasion.

Because of the weather, that night we could have scored any ticket we wanted for a normally sold out Broadway show, including the original "Chorus Line," which was at that time a yearlong wait to get a seat.

I had worked my contacts to get tickets to see Bette Midler at the Copacabana that night. This was three degrees of separation to Gloria Steinem who was one of two people responsible for getting us the tickets. It pays to have good friends who know the right people. Obviously, this was a hot show and, even on that night, a complete sell-out with not an empty seat in the house. The "Divine Ms. M" has major devotees and that night proved it. There was going to be NOTHING stopping me from attending that performance, and apparently everyone else with a ticket felt the same way.

When it came to performances, Bette was not the only show in town. The fashion magazine offices were also hives of activity as buyers, merchandisers and other wizards of the retail industry were bundled up in the latest looks and happy to be inside these warm designer-laden cocoons to learn about the next season's must-haves.

I could not resist tagging along with Susan to these hilarious presentations and I learned some very important information as a result. I learned that this year "fog was the new black" at one magazine and that "fashion would be taking its color direction from the birds" at another. At this magazine, the bird theme was supported by fabric swatches of every color and pattern imaginable covering the walls of a large room with a huge, freestanding, ornate birdcage with two white lovebirds inside creating an island centerpiece. Nibblies were being served and everyone in that room—except us—was not the slightest bit a twitter over any of it, giving a quick glance to the fabrics as they noshed on their little hors d'oeuvres. I'm not sure the birds got any real attention.

What more needs to be said?

Everything I saw that day, clad in my fire engine red Bloomingdale's snow boots that I had purchased a day before out of necessity, made it clear to me that my fashion office work was safely in the rearview mirror. I had enjoyed the first step of my career at the store, following every trend, and being the good soldier for years, but now I was comfortably into my favorite jeans and classic loafers, and I was planning on staying in them. A little birdie told me this would work out, and as it turned out, that little birdie was me. I found that jeans and loafers worked well wherever I went, and they still do.

Since I was now the mistress of my own fate, I could easily get away, as long as I had money, so I did a lot of traveling funded by my freelance writing gigs. Having the freedom to travel is definitely a great fringe benefit of freelance work and it certainly helped shape my career. Being exposed to other cultures can add so much to life overall and is especially helpful in marketing.

Although I was enjoying my life as a writer with wanderlust, I had to work, and as luck would have it I got a call from my friend, a local newspaper editor/publisher whom I had met as a result of my tenure in the fashion office. We had worked together on events at the store that her newspaper helped to promote. Maggi was well-known and a great promotional partner to the downtown retail business community, which was the newspaper's focus and forte. I had been a supporter of this paper by buying advertising in it for my clients so I was familiar with the product and knew its strengths.

Eight months after leaving the department store, after birthing a small freelance advertising business and taking a few trips here and there, I was hired as a sales representative for this publishing company. Although I had no experience in the newspaper business, I knew I could do well because the job was in sales.

Part of the deal I made with this publishing company was that my freelance business could continue, and that was a factor in my decision to accept the position. It was clear to me that this would benefit my clients, the paper and me. If my freelance client purchased space, I could produce that ad as a part of the deal through the newspaper's production department. So instead of paying for production somewhere else, my client paid for the space and got the production gratis.

Good things always happen when you think win-win rather than win-whatever.

Essentially my clients got the benefit of exposure by running ads for the price of producing them, and less than it would have cost them elsewhere. This was value-added for my client and increased revenue for the paper. More than likely my clients would not have run the ads had I not been involved because they didn't think they had the budget to do so.

I learned so much during my time at the newspaper. I upped my writing skills as a regular editorial contributor. I wrote several weekly columns on a variety of matters to include sports, travel, and other subjects I liked to pontificate about, and then I sold the advertising sponsorships necessary to support each column's existence. For example, I got one of the big banks in town to run an ad each week showing foreign currency conversions versus the dollar to support my travel column. The paper was full of advertising-supported content and my columns were no exception.

One of the people on my sales team was a woman who, over a very short period of time, became my best friend, a relationship that continues to this day. Sam is one of the most creative minds I have ever met and is an expert in sales. She's a natural. We teamed up on many schemes over the years beginning with many at this newspaper.

There was usually a large, overriding theme for each issue, bringing with it increased sales. My favorite of these strategic initiatives was our "salute" to a new store's grand opening. This mega promotion involved a major fashion retailer who was opening one of their flagship stores as the jewel in the crown of the newly renovated downtown core. Needless to say, it was a major event for the business and retail community, and our paper pulled out all the stops. The entire issue was dedicated to the opening.

This edition created additional revenue by way of selling ads to many companies congratulating this iconic fashion retailer. By now, I was the advertising director, managing a three-person team. We approached every vendor and subcontractor that had anything to do with this project to get them in on the action. We sold ads to the elevator and escalator companies, various construction companies, the electricians, the plumbing company, even to the guys who made the brass lettering that spelled out the company name on the side of the building. We sold ads to all their fashion vendors, too, all the companies whose products were carried by the store. No proverbial stone was left unturned. We sold them all, and it was a huge success on many levels.

The most profitable sale for me came as a result of approaching their competitors by offering them a listing on a two-page spread in the center of the issue with the headline banner: “Welcome, from your friends and neighbors.” The companies were listed alphabetically, their names included on the list for a mere $25. The major companies in town eagerly signed up, which included most local stores of note, top restaurants, major financial institutions, and the utility companies. There were about 150 companies represented on these pages. Every well-known entity in town participated with one exception: my old alma mater, the biggest department store in town.

Obviously, I contacted them first. There was the usual rigmarole—this one had to ask that one, and in the end, after many calls and attempts to get an answer, no one got back to me by the deadline. So they were not on the list. The paper was published as usual, coming out on Monday mornings in boxes all over town and delivered to a gratis subscriber base that included all the region’s top management. It was Monday morning at 10:00 a.m., just a few hours after this special salute-themed issue had been distributed, when I got a call from the President of the missing store on the list.

I had been introduced to him a few times, but we had never really spoken one on one. He asked me why his store had been left off the list. I explained to him that despite my numerous calls and attempts to get a green light through the appropriate channels, no one had bothered to call back. Insult was added to the injury when he was told the cost was $25 to be listed. He went silent on the other end of the line for a moment and then promised to get back to me shortly, once he spoke with his posse.

The story has a very happy ending. He did call back, just as he promised, but with a big present in his arms. He requested a 52-week, full page ad contract to be submitted to him immediately for his signature, a jewel of a sale that had eluded the newspaper until now. Bank error in my favor.

It was all made possible because the publisher knew a good idea when she heard one. She was not threatened by great ideas, no matter where they came from, including her staff. She is a terrific salesperson herself and she always led by example when it came to selling. I learned by watching Maggi, and she will always be one of the guiding forces of my career. "Call me anything, but call me" was her motto, and on this Monday morning, the call paid dividends for me and the paper.

There were other times during my years of service at this company when necessity was the mother of invention and I would make a sale in an unorthodox fashion. I sold advertising space in several different publications under the company banner to include one magazine centered on home décor.

I was involved in helping to sell advertising in many "special" editions that were very important to the bottom line: that is what made them special. Needless to say, we created a lot of "special editions."

There was a large roofing company in town that had always participated in the remodeling special editions. There were three of these created during the year. One time when I reached out to this company as usual, the owner seemed less than enthusiastic about signing his three-issue deal. He tried to get out of it gracefully, saying that he did not "think" he wanted to continue to participate but he did not want to be unsupportive either.

"Think" was the operative word I heard as he confessed that he was being pulled by two forces and was on the fence about what to do. I needed a plan immediately to get him off the fence and to sign the contract, so I told him that IF he agreed to run ONLY three more half page ads, one each in our next three "special" remodeling editions starting with this one, I would NEVER, EVER call him again.

He signed the contract and by doing so proved two of my theories: People give money to people they like, and you just have to make them an offer they can not refuse.

4

AD AGENCY BASICS

No Guts, No Green Stamps

If I had known early on what I know now, I still would have gone into business for myself. I never questioned the decision because it was a natural evolution and fit for me. It happened organically.

I tend not to let others take control of my life, especially when it comes to being creative. I never wait for someone to provide the platform. I go out seeking it. I need no outside authority, approval or encouragement beyond myself because as I have learned, opportunity is a gift you give yourself. Being creative is an essential part of my DNA, and I am always exploring and growing that part of myself to this day.

I knew my days at the newspaper were numbered, not only because I was ready to be my own boss, make my own rules or break them as required, but because I had landed a significant piece of business to handle the advertising of a regional 14-store junior and women's fashion chain. I could no longer spin two plates at once: a freelance business and a full-time job as advertising director at the weekly paper. It was time to dig deep, press the tab on my address book, and call for advice.

I called Fred, who was working for a worldwide ad agency. He had spent time in both their New York City offices and also abroad, and now was in the post of vice president at one of their satellite firms in town. I had called on this agency as a sales rep for the newspaper and sold them an ad or two. I respected them immensely.

Fred was a friend of Susan, my soon-to-be second agency partner. Even though I barely knew him, he seemed to know me and where I was in my thinking. I confided in him that I was content, but not challenged. I had my job at the paper down to a science and was making good money and freelancing on the side. He advised that I take one of two paths: either go to New York and become a cub copywriter and have a ball sweating it out paycheck to paycheck at first, or take my freelance business and run with it by opening my own agency.

I took a leap of faith and went forward with option two.

Even though I had some great opening acts in my career that taught me many things, when I opened my ad agency I had no idea what I was doing. I had no financial backing or traditional agency experience to mimic. It never crossed my mind that I couldn't do it either. I had the will and the desire to do it, and I made up my own rules as I went along based on common sense and great advice from my many partners in the process.

Over the years, I assembled a qualified team to do what I could not do myself, but only a few of them had any previous agency experience either. We always liked people who also liked out-of-the-box thinking. The best staff we had thrived in that environment, too. I never cared how long anyone worked. We had no timesheets. I only cared that they did a great job and were responsible for the activity they were charged with performing. If one could achieve greatness in a small amount of time, that was fine with me. Trust me when I tell you that this was a major motivator, and one of the fringe benefits of working at our company. We gave time off with pay regularly because our staff would do anything for us and our clients when the chips were down. It's a simple formula and it works.

A lack of experience did not inhibit our company from blossoming because authenticity and talent can be sold regardless of how much money is in the bank or how many awards or degrees hang on the walls.

Selling is the business of advertising at its core, and selling is my wheelhouse.

To quote Aristotle, "We are what we repeatedly do; excellence, then, is not an act, but a habit."

I was never asked about my experience or educational background prior to getting any client or project. Most of our clients rarely came to our offices, but when they did what they saw was comforting. Our offices were creative but humble. I always heeded the advice I got from one of my good friend's father who owned a very successful ad agency in San Francisco for many years. He told me not to have lavish offices because the clients would look around and say, "Who's paying for this?"

Getting those in the know to tell you what to do pays off, and when these teachers come along and impart their wisdom, strong listening skills are the key to maximizing that opportunity. I am also a major note taker.

Listening is the key to learning.

In this case I was listening to one of the best in my business and I would always bow to real-world advice. I'm a big talker but I can talk and listen at the same time. It's a skill that is culturally imbedded. I also learned early on that people give money to people they like. Having a sense of humor doesn't hurt, either.

In terms of gathering very talented and creative people, it all started when I convinced my first business partner to team up with me. She was a recent graduate of the local museum art school with a focus on fashion illustration. She had also done a stint in New York City at *Mademoiselle* magazine as a guest editor. She loved to draw, and clearly had a passion for it. Her education supported her innate talents but even better, she had great personal style and was very, very likeable. Deidre has the "it" factor. However, after a few years, she wanted a home life, and life as an agency owner was not fitting her needs. It was sad but in business, as in life, you have to roll with the changes.

My second partner, Susan, and I had a long history before she joined me at the agency. She was the former fashion merchandising director at the store where I cut my teeth, and had been my boss. We had become close friends through that experience and more. She had since retired from that post and was living the easier life as a free spirit—in a teepee no less—living on the proceeds of a fashion textbook she had authored. She was always a chameleon, transforming from her fashion costumes into hippie garb in the parking lot as she left the store for weekends in the wilderness. She went from the retail world to the natural world, from high heels to cowboy boots, until she retired and did the boots full time.

I convinced her that owning an ad agency was something she had to do because our client roster was growing and I needed her help handling it all. She had a fantastic work ethic and natural creative talents and we parlayed our joint experiences, personalities and skill sets working for many fashion retail businesses. We joined forces with a photographer who I had met and worked with in my days at the newspaper. In short order we added an office manager, production manager, copywriter, art director, and media buyer. We had the benefit of many creative and talented people as employees, freelance collaborators, and media sales reps and together we produced some great work.

Most of our clients were satisfied enough to stay with us for many years. We had relatively low client turnover even though turnover is always inevitable. The agency grew because when you produce results, performing as promised, clients usually stay put. However, sometimes it has nothing to do with performance. As in all areas of life, politics also come into play and clients sometimes come and go based on factors beyond your control.

It is important to be able to pick up and move on. You can't take things personally, and you must realize there are more opportunities in the sea. This is one of the reasons why selling is the whole shooting match. Regardless of the reason, if one client leaves, you have to be able to reel in another.

It is still magic to me when advertising works. Every time a campaign produced results I would say, "oh yes, I knew it would," all the while thinking to myself, "thank God it did!"

I believe that business is the finest form of art. You just have to have good instincts and believe something will happen before it actually does. You have to take chances and operate accordingly so you have no regrets. When it comes to strategy I always begin with the end in mind and apply equal amounts of fairness and logic to whatever I do.

Marketing is always a gamble, an art, not a science.

Advertising is a business in which yesterday means nothing. Retail sales are viewed in comparison to last year's figures, but in advertising the rule is you are only as good as the last campaign. The weather, economic conditions, competitive factors, bad merchandise—none of it matters. You are judged each time, and when things do not go as planned, you wonder if there was more you could have done, even though you thought you gave your all. Was there a better creative strategy or a more effective media plan?

We also did return to seek more counsel from my early advisor, the seasoned advertising veteran. Not only had he advised me to open the agency but now he had more wonderful suggestions on how to cope in the agency business and deal with clients and their issues. He was qualified to do this because he had spent most of his career in account management. He was a fountain of wisdom and penned many jewels that I have used ever since. Two of my favorites are "there is no logic in owning a dog and barking yourself," and "I don't have to make that decision now." I can't say how many times I have quoted him, using these two phrases to get myself down off the ceiling or out from hiding under my desk.

The best advice I can give to someone contemplating opening a marketing business is to ask lots of questions from people who really know their stuff, but all the while remember that it is only their opinion. It's a balancing act of following those in the know and making the rules as you go along to best suit your needs. You need to surround yourself with the best team possible to support you in the areas where you are not best qualified, then go boldly forward. Whether you have been there before or not, always focus on contributing your best talents and showcasing others' skills in concert.

The old line is true: When you do what you love, money will follow. However, in the end, self-confidence and guts are what matter most, and are more important than working capital because that is the order in which they materialize.

5

UNDERSTANDING NUMBERS

Statistics Lie

Apparently, I was always good with numbers. In fact, early on in my life, and to my surprise, I got a higher SAT score in math than English. I was always in accelerated English classes in high school, and I got consistently high marks and I also struggled in math—so go figure. This is when I first learned that sometimes numbers don't matter most, or reflect reality.

I know that numbers are used to prove almost every theory, yet they often prove nothing essential and that is why they are not reliable in forming a conclusion. Have you ever heard of a long shot winning a race? In the end, the horse with the worse odds surprises the crowd with the victory. Some people are not surprised, having bet on that long shot, and they cash in big. Some people just have good intuition, or dare I say luck, and they run with it.

Luck comes to those who are best prepared, as the saying goes. Sometimes you have to think your way to winning and listen to and trust your inner voice.

This doesn't stop the data zealots from spreading meaningless conclusions. These people want you to hang onto

every fraction, but I suggest that when it comes to marketing effectiveness, numbers often require a closer look and an ability to see through them to do what really counts.

Buying advertising time and space can be based solely on numbers if you listen to the media. Broadcasters (radio, TV or digital) want you to believe that their statistics, called ratings and shares, clicks or hits, followers or thumbs-up, are the truth and matter because they help direct ad dollars to media coffers. The ad industry uses elaborate theories of analysis that are actually, more often than not, estimates. Almost everyone in the media buying business accepts and studies these numbers like nobody's business, and use them to make their decisions to determine what programs, platforms, periodicals, and stations will be purchased. Most importantly, these stats also determine the cost to run an ad and the higher the number, the higher the price to purchase. However, when the numbers are high, it is not always the right time to buy.

TV contests such as “American Idol,” “The Voice,” or “Dancing with the Stars” often crown champions by call-in votes. These are often based solely on popularity rather than who is really the best. Jennifer Hudson came in sixth place on “Idol” but we can see how wrong the numbers were in her case. Her success proves otherwise.

Numbers from diaries, electronic devices called ‘people meters,” or phone research are not exact sciences. If the TV is on does that mean that someone is watching? And if someone is watching, who is that? If the radio is on, does that mean anyone is listening? Not necessarily. If one is online, or looking through a magazine, do they read any of the ads? You don’t have to be a media buyer to reach the obvious conclusions.

Numbers also provide a convenient cover if things do not go as planned. The fact is advertising effectiveness has more to do with creative concept and execution than anything else.

Newspapers and magazines rely on numbers of subscribers; however many of their readers receive gratis copies that they did not ask for. Do they read the content or do they skim the headlines or flip through the pages looking at photos, sometimes in a waiting room at their doctor’s office or elsewhere? Some subscribers get the periodical but never open the copy even if they purchased it.

Who knows who actually has seen or absorbed anything?

Outdoor advertising is sold based on traffic counts or how many vehicles are driving by a billboard or wallscape. The numbers do not measure or reflect who are in the vehicles or if any of those on the move are the target audience.

When it comes to picking outdoor space, the conventional wisdom has always been to pick the locations with the most traffic. I never subscribed to this strategy.

The most traffic is often found on Interstate highways, but when you put your message there, you are paying for many eyeballs passing through, many of whom will not be a customer for most locally marketed goods and services. This is good for a national or regional branding campaign, but most advertising is local and I always look for locations that have high impact with my client's primary audience. Sometimes a fantastic location with major visual impact did not have the highest traffic count and it was priced less as a result. In the end, I deliver more impact for a lower out-of-pocket cost.

Most customers live within five miles of a business they frequent.

For these reasons, when it comes to buying media, I do not make numbers my focus. This is not how I approach it. I do not spend my time and energy poring over data and I don't really care what the ratings are, or what share of the audience a show, station, periodical, or platform enjoys according to the data. These are not my primary concerns. I just use common sense and my third eye.

I can tell early on what will be a hit or miss because I read, watch, and listen to judge media in action for myself. I can tell what is hot or not in short order because I stay tuned into popular culture and trends. I trust my instincts because I am the chief shopper so how I think usually matters. I regularly deliver a better media mix with better returns for less money because I am buying before any numbers show up. You have to have the guts to do what often is not supported by the numbers. Statistics are late to the party, and slow to materialize.

Operating with good instincts and common sense, rather than following the numbers, delivers savings and creates better ability to reach an audience. When something is hot, the cost is often too high. Buy low, not high is my motto when I go shopping for media with my client's dollar.

You always pay more for being a follower.

I am always on the lookout for opportunities. A great example of this was when Oprah first came on to national syndicated TV. I knew instantly that she would be a huge success. It was clear to me that if someone was giving this woman, who very few people knew of at the time, a daily weekday talk show, she must be the Second Coming. I quickly hopped onto her train and negotiated one commercial a day for a year for one of my clients on the first station to carry her show. The price was very low because no one had any idea of the success she would enjoy.

In this case, I worked with, and purchased this media buy through a regional rep firm. Shortly after the order was placed and Oprah had been on the air for only three weeks, I was informed by my rep that the general sales manager of that station had returned my approved purchase order with a message on it saying, "when is this f---ing deal over?"

Turned out Oprah was the Second Coming and this was

three weeks into a secured annual contract.

It was a similar situation with "The Joan Rivers Show." Once I heard Joan was coming back on TV after her "Tonight Show" snub, I did not hesitate to buy commercials on her show for my clients. Although it was a different scenario, I reached the same conclusion because I did not need numbers to convince me that I should get on board quick. I knew Joan would deliver, and she did. Joan also took the time and effort to thank me personally, while Oprah did not but I do not hold that against her.

I have used the same strategy over and over with all my media campaigns and the result is always the same. I get more bang for my client's buck. You have to use common sense, believe in yourself, and trust your instincts. To be successful in marketing you need the courage of your convictions.

In the advertising business you must learn that no matter how high the ratings, how high the traffic count, how large the circulation, or how many clicks or hits, the only numbers that really matter are the sales figures. When they are up, it doesn't matter who is watching, reading, or listening to the ads. When sales are down, it also doesn't matter that the number of viewers, readers or listeners, are up or down.

The one place where statistics always count is the results—the bottom line—and that lesson I learned during my days in retail. It was the old 3 p.m. cash register reading that determined whether it was a good day or not. The money in the till tells the story. That is still my orientation, and I never lose sight of that prize. Increases in performance are great, but being up over last year—if last year was a disaster—is nothing to write home about. Statistics may lie, results never do.

To be successful, focus your attention on the right target. I always direct my attention to the "chief shopper." If you want to know what she is watching, listening to, or reading, all you have to do is ask her, or better still witness her in action. Either way, she will tell you what you need to know. All you have to do is ask the right people the right questions. This requires a healthy curiosity, a good memory and patience in order to get to the bottom of it. You have to know how to connect with women and get them to tell you the truth. It definitely helps to be a woman.

Eighty percent of all goods and services are purchased by women 40 years or older. This group may not be the funding source for everything they buy, but they are the one doing the purchasing. In other words, they decide what to buy and where. Recently, *The New York Times* ran a front page story about advertisers coming back to this audience after chasing other demographic groups. I knew this decades ago. I saw it when women were the audience for the menswear fashion shows I was involved in during my early days in retail. Women buy more men's products than men do.

Since I am one of these chief shoppers, demographically speaking, when I purchase advertising I consider what I would do or watch, or listen to, or read. I am usually the "she" I am looking to reach.

Besides my own instincts, I routinely reach out to women of all ages to ask them what they think about any number of subjects. I like to engage different females while they are in the process of consuming or buying something because then the commentary is supported by action. Once you get talking, they tell you everything. It definitely helps to have the gift of gab.

Sometimes I will make a statement about how I feel about something to see another woman's reaction, to see if she feels as I do. Most of the time we agree, but if we don't I take note. For example, how does she feel about being approached to donate to a charity at the checkout counter in the grocery store? How does she feel about self-service, unsolicited mail or too many choices? Best time to find out is when it is actually happening rather than waiting to see their opinion on a survey later on. The answer you get later may or may not be the truth because people often do not like to admit their true feelings in writing if they think it is not the way they should be feeling. Some people are ashamed to admit that they do not like something or do not know how they actually feel. Some people are insecure about their opinions.

If you ask someone to complete a survey voluntarily, with or without a financial incentive, store discount or other "gift" as bait, only the truly committed will do so. Shrinking violets will not participate, but shrinking violets are a large part of the primary shopper group. Perhaps busy people or those not motivated by money will not participate either. Gift certificate redemption is actually lower than you think; this is a clue about money being the top motivator. "Had what I wanted" is the number one reason for shopping somewhere, not cost or convenience.

Since 90% of all communication is nonverbal, face to face interaction will always trump theoretical research. Marry that to this statistic: 80% of a company's sales usually come from just

20% of their customers so it is vital to be looking at the right target and their opinions. Only a very small sample of consumers are often represented in market research findings based on many factors, some of which I have touched on here.

One of my favorite places to conduct face-to-face market research is in the grocery store, often in the paper products aisle. I always find some frustrated-looking woman trying to figure out what is the best buy in paper towels or toilet paper, using her less-than-stellar math skills to determine the best deal. Since I think this is an exhausting process myself, I relate to her mission, and there is simpatico. After a few comments, I can quickly ask her a few media questions.

Often we are on the same page. Her media choices are no surprise to me. I talk to enough women that I have a pretty good idea of this group's likes and dislikes. It doesn't take too many responses to determine a trend which leads to a conclusion. As long as you know your target, this is far more determinative than poring over the media numbers.

Malls use traffic counters to determine the value of real estate. Mall owners love to tell their retail tenants how much traffic the mall is delivering, and they get these numbers from counters embedded in the floors near the entrances. What does this mean? Very little unless you dig deeper, and you can't do that because the counters just register footprints. So if a busload of seniors arrive at a mall and they walk around for exercise and buy nothing more than a cup of coffee, why do we care how many came on that bus unless you are selling coffee? It is the same story with teenagers who meet at a mall to socialize. Yes, they all may buy something to eat but how important is the headcount if I am selling clothes to woman over 35?

On the web, a zillion "friends" or "followers" make some people feel important and connected, but often they are neither. It makes for interesting conversation, but do the numbers really matter? If website traffic counts were reliable from a marketing perspective, web-based advertising would be the road to riches for all, and the only advertising anyone would ever do. The companies who took this approach would all be knee-deep in profits but unfortunately, it's not that simple.

**In both advertising and retail,
traffic does not guarantee sales.**

When it comes to buying anything—including advertising media—it is important to work with the best salespeople. They know their numbers and can give you that overview. If they are good, you can trust their advice. Again, observational skills are important when deciding who to do business with in the media world. I have always weeded out the best people to work with in partnership and to have on my team. Conveniently, these people also tended to work for the best media companies, too.

So Grandma, your theory works! Forget about the numbers because you will reach the "promised land" when you just buy the best.

Part Two
Experience

6
MEDIA BUYING

Nothing Sells like Television

One of my favorite yarns is a story about one of my experiences involving television advertising.

I was first sold on TV as the best way to advertise from Dusty, who turned out to be a significant mentor and my first television rep. She had done a stint as a station business manager, and she impressed me on many levels. She later became my one of my confidantes, helping me in every way imaginable. She helped me financially in more ways than one and became a client, lender, and counselor in my early days. Most importantly, she became a real friend and I trusted her judgment totally.

Her final coup in the TV business was becoming a business manager again for a larger station. Part of her responsibility was to act as the general contractor for the station's new high-rise headquarters in the center of the city. It was a major undertaking, and she was up to the task. After the project was completed, she ended up retiring from the media business to help a nonprofit organization effectively distribute donations to the needy in Africa. Like I said before, she made a strong impression on me, and for many good reasons.

TV as a media choice just made the most sense to me. I knew people do not generally have good listening skills and often do not retain what they do hear. Most people are better watchers than listeners, and better at watching anything than doing most anything. TV works two senses, so it gets to you one way or the other. This is why TV is still one of the best ways to advertise, and one of the most powerful ways to present an image. Video communication has endured from its inception as multiple delivery systems continue to evolve and offer more options for viewing.

The average American watches four to five hours of TV a day. Seniors watch an average of seven to eight hours a day, and that includes the president.

Despite the many ways to see programming, and no matter what time of day or night they are viewed, there are still TV shows that have enormous and loyal audiences. "The Bachelor/Bachelorette" franchise spawned Bachelor Nation. Companies across the country take a break every day to watch "Ellen." Soap operas that have been on the air for decades or the latest must-see shows such as "The Walking Dead," "Empire," "The Kardashians," or "Modern Family" prove that network TV still delivers big, and consistently so. YouTube, Netflix, and all the other digital platforms drive even more viewing. Of course, TV also drives our political landscape, which in turn, affects our culture overall.

Years ago my agency did a campaign for a large hospital chain. The goal was to get seniors to switch to the hospital's HMO for free health care. It is not an easy task to get older people to switch doctors. The first thing that came to my mind was that my grandmother had her television set insured, which meant that in case it broke down, she would get a loaner while it was being fixed. She did this to make sure that she would never miss her beloved soap operas. TV programming was that essential to her lifestyle and happiness. This was all I really needed to know in order to develop a media strategy for this client project.

Initially, when I recommended a television campaign, the client did not understand why TV would be better than newspaper to reach the target audience. They had seen "the numbers," and that was that. Without the boring details, it was a long battle, but I fought the law and the law didn't win.

I placed a three-week TV schedule, and after three days the program had been completely filled up with the number of participants they hoped for. Based on the success of the strategy, they ended up extending the enrollment opportunity to allow more seniors to join and we extended the TV campaign to support this second membership drive. They reached their second-round goal as well. This was the first time this national health organization did television advertising anywhere and because the program was special and supported by the federal government, it was under the microscope, to say the least. In the end, and presumably based on the success of our campaign, it was not the last time they used TV either. They did it big time and nationwide.

I would often get client referrals from my media partners, especially from my TV reps. Salespeople liked referring business to me, companies who were looking for advertising assistance, because they hoped I would land the account. If I did, it would mean new business for them. They knew I loved TV because it worked and because “new business” is next to godliness in sales; when this occurred it was another win-win arrangement.

One of my favorite TV stories began with a referral to a local restaurant chain consisting of six pizza parlors. They were looking to grow to 25 locations. The CEO was the matriarch of her family business, with her son acting as executive vice president of marketing. We made plans to meet but since this was a food account, I knew I would have to taste their offerings before agreeing to represent them because I must always believe completely in what I am selling.

I went to sample the goods. I took my associate with me so there would be two opinions. Unfortunately, we both hated the pizza and to make matters worse, there were cinnamon rolls sitting next to the pizza on their self-service buffet like two jewels in their crown, which made me wonder if this was all the same dough in two configurations and with different toppings.

I tasted both and I think that it might have been true.

I could see that there were too many titled decision makers in this kitchen and the recipes were not to my liking so I knew that this was not a fit.

To be polite, I kept the meeting and planned to make it short and sweet dispensing a sprinkling of my usual "free advice." I wanted them to be left with a good taste in their mouth even though I hadn't and to show respect for my rep who recommended me.

The CEO and her son the EVP were both there for the meeting and very firmly planted in their thinking. They had little experience in marketing and clearly did not have a head for it from where I sat across the booth from them. They had no clue about how to build their brand from my perspective and were looking to hire followers who would just do what they had already decided to do.

I told them they needed to use TV if they wanted to expand their chain and grow, but they adamantly resisted the idea. They had already decided to use radio as their medium of choice. So, I kept it light, bright and tight and wished them the best of luck, all the while thinking how glad I was not to have to deal with them. I sent a short but sweet thanks but no thanks letter and wrote it off as more fodder for a book one day.

Voila! The day has come, and now for the rest of the story. The plot sickens.

Roughly 10 years later, it came to pass that the TV stations in my city decided to form a consortium to fund a new marketing effort to promote television advertising. They decided to hire an agency to give them a professional outside opinion. Of all the agencies in town they could have chosen, they hired me. This was a big honor for a small boutique shop like mine, to be selected over all the larger marketing companies available for this assignment, the ones who were responsible for directing the majority of revenue to these stations. Of course, I knew how to sell TV quite well, and had demonstrated this repeatedly over the years but this was my golden rule coming to life once again. I always believe that people give money to people they like and these people liked me. The feeling was mutual.

The consortium consisted of all four network affiliates in the market—ABC, CBS, FOX, NBC—and the one major independent station. First order of business was to develop a plan that would determine the target. Industries were selected because they were either currently underspending on TV advertising or they had potential to become major TV advertisers. These sectors included a variety of industries such as real estate, banks, health care, automotive, and restaurants.

I came up with the idea that, in the consortium's behalf, I would conduct market research in the form of informational interviews. These were conducted with significant players in these targeted industries in an effort to determine how they actually made decisions regarding their advertising strategy and media choices. We also wanted to find out who was on their buying committees. There are always many stakeholders with opinions and input.

These interviews helped develop the strategy that turned into a video magazine series distributed to all advertising decision makers, top agency management, and in-house marketing chiefs alike. These videos were distributed over a short period of time, a different one every few weeks. Each video featured three well-known personalities who were successful TV advertisers from the targeted sectors. The result was a strong message delivered directly from significant industry leaders explaining how effective TV had been for growing their companies and establishing their brands.

If you want to know what people are really thinking, you just have to ask the right questions.

It was a very successful campaign for the television industry. The president of one of the largest ad agencies on the list sent a letter to all the TV station general managers in the group proclaiming the video series as "the best use of marketing dollars ever seen from the TV industry." I was very happy to add this project to my resume and our agency portfolio.

I got a special bonus from this activity as well. It came time to feature the restaurant category, and a familiar name popped up on the list of potential TV success stories and interestingly enough, it was someone I had met before. Lo and behold, it was the CEO of that pizza chain I had walked away from many years before. I wasn't too surprised that she made the list because she was all over the air with her commercials, and she was the star of the show promoting her pizza and cinnamon rolls. I was always amused when I saw them, and seeing the numbers of her stores escalate as a result built my confidence too.

I showed up with my camera crew, as usual, to get the interview down on tape. This time the location was, of course, at one of her restaurants which by now were a household name. Every time I saw her commercials I thought back to that day when I told her to use TV instead of radio as she resisted. The radio campaign was now nowhere to be heard or remembered, but she was a major fixture on TV, a success story for the record, and a well-known local character because of it.

She did not recognize me, which I found hilarious since I looked pretty much the same as the day we met, and here I thought I was memorable! Not missing a beat, I conducted the interview and she crowed on and on about her success with TV. When the interview was over, I said to her, "Did you know that we have met before? And do you know when that was?" She was a deer in the headlights. After I explained the circumstances of our first meeting and reminded her of my recommendation to use television, it confirmed what I suspected all along. She was not a good listener and the reason she was not listening was because her mind was made up before we met. I was not telling her what she wanted to hear so she probably tuned me out. She could have been more successful sooner had she listened to someone with advertising experience. She didn't realize that listening is the key to learning.

The big lesson here is you should know what business you are in and stay focused on your unique contribution to the overall cause. Even if you are an expert in one business, this does not qualify you to automatically be an expert in another.

Marketing is a large umbrella consisting of many parts—advertising, sales, public relations, publicity and product development. People who have professional marketing careers are part of a team; they are specialists in their craft if they are really good at what they do. It is not possible to be good at everything in the world of marketing or any other world for that matter, and definitely not if you already have the job of CEO.

7

CREATIVE DIRECTION

I'm Not Wild about Harry

I remember the first time someone asked me if I could create a radio spot for his business. Fortunately, I had three radio veterans on my team so I said "yes, no problem" because it wasn't. Creating commercials was never an issue because I had such talented friends. Surrounding yourself with creative thinkers pays dividends.

This request came from a guy who owned a great little shoe store. He had an unusual last name and we played off it, and since he had both good self-esteem and sense of humor, he loved it. We created a campaign of fractured fairy tales where shoes were the key element of the storyline—think Cinderella and glass slippers.

The commercials we created were always memorable—funny and smart. Our voice talent was second to none. In this case they were two of the best I have ever heard, one a very experienced reporter, TV anchor and radio news director, and the other a top deejay who ended up as production manager for one of the largest media conglomerates in the business. At this time, David and Michael were working together as morning drive partners at a radio station. Needless to say, they had the skills to do the job. My only challenge was that they were 325 miles away, so the copy was given to them over the phone because this was the era of no fax or email. They would cut the commercial late at night, after hours, and then send the tape to me via the bus the following day. I just did whatever I had to do to deliver the best product for my clients.

As with every advertising campaign I was ever involved in, it was often the clients that made it tough. They behaved as if they thought "this is fun, looks easy enough, I can do it." But they couldn't do it well and that is why they hired people who could.

Some people do not understand the "approve or disapprove, not improve" rule. Creativity done by committee is difficult enough when everyone has the talent, but impossible when someone gets involved who is not capable yet thinks they are.

There is no logic in owning a dog and barking yourself, as my consultant Fred told me years ago.

After the shoe store, another one of my first radio campaigns was for a guy named Harry. This one was a royal challenge. He was very accomplished as a retailer and had very good taste in goods, but he was the type who thought he was always the best at everything.

It turned out that Harry didn't have it all figured out after all. Turned out that he didn't anticipate the success of our radio campaign that we executed for his kitchenware store and delicatessen.

The spots were all about bringing customers into his store, and specifically to his deli. The campaign was so successful that in record time he had quite a crowd in the deli and his crew was not prepared or able to keep up with the increased demand. He called me up in a panic, asking if we could take the spots off the air. This is akin to buying a bunch of food for a party and then right before the expiration date on the products asking the store to take the food back for a full refund. What could a store do with these products at that point? Nothing.

Understanding what it is like to be on the other side of the fence is fundamental for great business relationships.

Had the store been able to sell the goods for the past few weeks, they probably could have sold them. It's a fair comparison, expecting to get out of a campaign at the last minute. The station is left with that inventory and cannot sell the airtime because campaigns are placed well in advance and seldom is some advertiser sitting around with extra budget to burn at the last minute.

Anyway, back to solving the issue at hand. Harry was not

one of those win-win thinkers. He thought he could just cancel as a way to get out of his fix because the campaign was working too well. I said no can do, for the reason already explained. However, I did want to resolve the issue amicably to everyone's satisfaction.

I told him that we would come up with another commercial simply asking the customers to leave. We would plug his takeout business with the immortal line rewritten as follows: "Please come into our deli and buy our fantastic meats and cheeses, fine wines, great hors d'oeuvres, our imported beers—and then, GO HOME! Take home our fantastic meats and cheeses, fine wines, great hors d'oeuvres, our imported beers." We just amended our original pitch and added the "go home" spin, reversing our message, and it worked again like a charm. Harry got business and the station got theirs. Problem solved.

The lesson here is, don't ever kill a golden goose just find a way to satisfy all the palates.

8

ESTABLISHING STANDARDS

You're Done NOT Listening to Me

When it comes to clients, you have to know when to fight and when to switch. To quote my mom, "when to hold 'em, when to fold 'em, when to walk away" is what you must have in your arsenal. I would like to illustrate the "when to walk away" option with the following tale.

There was a local family business that had been selling men's clothing for many, many years. When the founder, the father, was alive, my best recollection of the store was that it sold mostly shirts and ties. There were always zillions of them in the window displays.

When his son took over the business the store changed. He made it very upscale and started catering to both men and women. To this day, the company carries a beautiful selection of clothes, only the best and at high prices.

When it came to marketing he acted like a jack of all trades, and it turned out that his lack of marketing expertise stopped a lot of creativity from manifesting for his company. It certainly did with us, and I don't think we were the only ones. There seemed to be a lack of trust and respect for that type of experience by others. He did not know what business he was in, and thought he could have several brilliant careers at once, never realizing how unrealistic that mindset can be. He acted as though he was an expert in advertising, and he assumed that anyone with creative talent in one arena could be successful in another without much effort or dues paid. Bottom line was that he could not be satisfied with perfecting his craft—the art of merchandising—and in doing so, never benefited from many others who do likewise in a different arena.

I knew it was time to resign the account after I presented a creative concept that was perfect in every way based on the challenge he presented to us. He wanted us to develop a multi-media image campaign that would serve two different purposes simultaneously. One use would be to promote the grand opening of this company's first store in another major metropolitan market, and at the same time also work as a Christmas holiday campaign in its home base. The two market areas are 165 miles away from each other and do not share common media.

The owner spent major dollars on food and beverage for the grand opening and, as always, pulled out all the stops to ensure that they had the very best merchandise available. However, the buck stopped there before any advertising budget could be presented. It was quickly concluded that the company could only afford one creative idea to be produced, so it had to support both grand opening and holiday.

At this time, a major architectural marvel was unfolding in the store's home city. The creation of a dynamic building, not far from the store, was about to be dedicated. The building was a new city complex, very controversial because of its unique and whimsical design created by a very famous, world class architect. Topping the project off was the second-largest bronze sculpture in the country which was to be placed a few stories above the main entrance. They brought this incredible piece of art by barge down the river that flows through the center of the city. The whole town was agog over it.

The Portland Building

Now back to the owner of the store who had casually mentioned to me in passing that this same famous architect had been in the city on several occasions, presumably to check on the status of the building project. Most recently he was in town due to its upcoming dedication, planned to occur just prior to the upcoming holiday season. In fact, my client said proudly that he "purchased some clothes at the store."

The stars had aligned for a perfect opportunity, so naturally when I heard this I was elated and somewhat relieved. In record time, I contacted that architect, Michael Graves, by phone in his office in Princeton, New Jersey, and presented my idea. Could he, would he, please agree to stand on the top of his building when he came back to town wearing the clothes he purchased at this store for our campaign we wanted to do? This would run in two cities simultaneously with the headline: “Testing the City Limits.”

This was an early example of how I was able to get people to do things I knew could be done if the situation was right. I was never afraid to ask anyone for help and as I had hoped, he agreed to do it. I love to think big.

I told him I would get back to him as soon as possible to firm up the details and thanked him profusely for agreeing to take part. I could not wait to present the strategy.

Unfortunately, my client did not see the merits of this idea. His exact words were, “I really don’t get the connection.” When he said those words I thought to myself, “I do,” and our business connection ended in that moment, even though it took a day longer to send the official Dear John letter of resignation.

I felt great about sending that letter. I would miss the income, but even worse, I had to call Mr. Graves back to say we were not going to do the campaign after all. I was very disappointed not to have been able to execute what I thought would be a perfect creative solution.

What I learned from this experience is you have to know when to hold ’em, when to fold ’em, and when to walk away. Right, mom?

9

ART VS. SCIENCE

Throw Mamas from the Train

I had a client who I knew quite well. We met in a totally different universe when I was a junior in high school. He was my journalism teacher and Mike was always a big fan of mine.

Over two consecutive years, I was the art editor and business editor of the school yearbook. My job was to design the book one year and then, in year two, manage a team in order to sell advertising to the local businesses in the school's orbit. This would bring in the necessary revenue required to support the creation of the book. It was clear from the start that I was better as a sales manager than as an art director but still, in a nutshell, those two years were a definite precursor to my career.

We had a nice student/teacher relationship. Mike was a young teacher who was a lot of fun, and he made the process of putting out the annual very entertaining. Not surprisingly, I got straight A's from him, term after term, not only because he liked me but because I earned each and every one of them.

Now fast forward 10 years later when my teacher ran into an old friend of mine from high school who was also a former student of his, another one of his favorites, who had been on the school newspaper staff. While reminiscing, Mike asked John if he knew what I was up to, and he was told that I had opened an ad agency. At that time, coincidentally, Mike was working for a company in major need of some serious marketing support, and when he found out that I had an agency, he thought I might be able to help him. Phone numbers were exchanged and the rest is history.

I was contacted, and then hired almost immediately to help him grow this company that he worked for, a regional chain of nine, for-profit business colleges. Years later, having risen to CEO, he ended up purchasing the company, expanding the network of schools in the US and Canada, growing to 14 campuses in 13 different market areas. The overall census grew from 2200 to 5300 students during the years we were responsible for their advertising.

In addition to the annual student census increases we delivered we helped the company to execute a system-wide corporate name change campaign. At times, this was like pulling teeth because the schools all bore their original college names, identities they had had since their inception. These monikers had been around for as long as 90 years in one case, the majority of them for 25 to 40 years.

The campaign required major public relations efforts inside the company and out. Let's just say there was the usual resistance to change so the job was no cakewalk.

All these name change challenges took place in addition to the ongoing image building and lead generation efforts and campaigns executed by our team. The chain was well-known as a result of our advertising successes, and an entire sales category of proprietary schools was born at the radio and TV stations. This was another win-win for the broadcasters and for our firm. I was known as a Pied Piper and I think I was routinely rewarded with value added promotions and airtime as a result. After all, my media partners were happy and they were happy to return favors.

I simply applied the same formula for this group of schools as I always had done with all of my clients. This means working hand in hand with the media, often broadcasters, to get the maximum exposure with the budgets given. I always operate with the idea that there are two mouths to feed and relished my role in bringing people together for mutual benefit. I always remember I have two partners in the dance.

My strategy is always crafted around the idea that everybody wins.

Since I know what to buy, and do so before the numbers back the decision, my clients get a much bigger bang for their buck and the media reps don't have to go through torture to get an order. They don't have to wait for the ratings to justify the purchase of their inventory. I also helped them build a new category of business for their stations.

Mike never stopped providing a classroom for me to learn

and grow. By representing his company, I was taught many lessons and my talents blossomed in that environment. It was here I learned the value of always keeping one's eye on the leads.

To that end, in concert with others on the corporate marketing team, we developed a lead control system and kept track of all 14 schools inquiries. We issued monthly reports on all lead activity and the enrollments that came as a result by source. We tracked all contacts coming into each school. There were over 20 different source codes including TV, radio, newspaper, trade shows, high school classroom presentations, yellow pages, and all types of referrals in addition to several catchall categories like "local knowledge." Thankfully, in those days, the internet was not in play, which would have only made the whole shebang that much more complicated.

This system would have been totally reliable had these prospects actually remembered what really made them initiate contact with the school, how and when they actually first heard of the school, but the majority really could not remember. It was often many reasons they made the call but there were also clues about what was really working.

Often, we would have people claiming that they had just seen our TV ads when we had been off the air for weeks and local knowledge or friend referral claims would increase during and in concert with major on-air TV flights.

The lead control system was developed because the client was always trying to make an art into a science and what they actually ended up with was a bunch of statistics that made them feel better about the advertising money they were spending. It was a constant battle to remind management not to run with lead numbers as gospel and to focus on the bottom line: enrollments. They were always trying to connect one action to a corresponding ad. If only life were like this, I would tell them.

However, having said all that, the lead generation program we instituted and managed for this school chain was another win-win arrangement. They were happy with their statistics, no matter if they were fact or fiction and we were happy to play along because the leads were always up over last year and so were total enrollments and those were the only statistics that really mattered to me.

Our message was often served up in testimonial format and while filming the commercials our role model students said, on camera, that they had seen the ads here, there, and everywhere. This supported our claim that there were many overlapping reasons that these students were impacted, prior to enrolling, by our campaigns. TV was ALWAYS on the list, which was not surprising because this is the medium that received the lion's share of the media budget. Because TV got the most absolute dollars, the medium was also always on the hot seat for producing big results.

We would show the testimonial outtakes of students explaining how they found out about the school to the executive committee and at sales meetings. This supported our rationale and strengthened our claims that our media strategy was working well. I must confess that serving up crow was always one of my favorite things to do when clients would question our abilities.

There were some people in the schools who were not as

happy with our success as we were, due to the scrutiny they were receiving as we tried to get to the bottom of how many leads were actually coming their way. All the inquiries were supposed to be counted, but we could often tell when that was not occurring because the stats coming back to us were questionable. Regularly, I would have a member of my staff call the schools and masquerade as a potential student or parent of a student, engage the admissions representative in dialogue to make sure things were happening as they should. We would then check to see if this "fake lead" would end up on the master log for that day. Often it did not, and then we knew we had a rat in our maze.

The next step would be to send a member of the company's marketing team out in the field to personally investigate the discrepancy matter. It should have been a clue to the school director when he or she would learn that Kelly was coming to town. Kelly was an ace investigator and equally committed to success. She had also been a top admissions producer so she knew the drill first-hand.

Sometimes it is about numbers because if you have 10 leads and enroll one student, you are closing at 10%. However, if you actually have 20 leads and enroll one student, that number is 5%. Counting leads was not a choice, but it did not stop them from trying to make it so. Several of the campuses were underreporting their numbers and that meant exaggerating their performance. This was very interesting to observe, both politically and sociologically speaking.

One campus that had been in our crosshairs was led by a woman who was a country and western singer on the side. She was a kick in the pants from our perspective, calling herself Mama.

However, her school was not honest in their reporting and so our secret campaign to get her replaced was referred to as "throw mama from the train."

She was not the only thorn in our side, or target in our mission to clean up the deception. Another was the acting queen bee of the company, or so she thought. This woman was the leader of the largest school in the chain, and was constantly deriding our efforts and undermining our strategy at every turn. We dubbed her demise "the last empress" because her school was in the market area known as "The Inland Empire." In the end, she left with her crown in her hand after we uncovered almost 1000 uncounted leads in her reps' desk drawers. They were working the leads, just not counting them all.

This business grew each year from the time me and mine came on board. For most of the 12 years we represented this company as their agency of record; the experience was very rewarding and we crafted a brand identity that was a leader in the industry, in the markets where they operated and, in most cases, with increasing competition from national companies with deeper pockets. We achieved our objectives and outdid ourselves year after year as the thank you holiday letter from Mike got longer and longer, accolades aplenty. It was a lovefest while it lasted.

And then the tide turned, as all tides invariably do.

I could see the handwriting on the wall. The colleges were not increasing enrollment as fast as they had been due to factors outside our jurisdiction and beyond our control, such as increasing government financial aid regulations. When Mike chose to fire one of the best minds in the business, his VP of Marketing, falsely making him the scapegoat, I knew we would be next. The company was struggling largely due to sea changes in the industry, and management was looking for someone to blame. They mistakenly believed that this move would be a life preserver, but it wasn't.

There are always changes in the marketplace that affect a company. Mike chose to listen to those on his team who were not marketers and in doing so, backed the wrong horses. As a result, he hired another agency and in short order, the company went out of business. I was not surprised at this outcome, but sad nonetheless.

I could read the nonverbal and indirect communication that gave clues to what lied ahead. It is advised to pay attention to these and accept the reality of a changing tide. No matter how secure you think your relationship is, or how long your history together, or how great your contributions have been, things change. Accept it as gracefully as possible and move on.

The old adage is always true: When one door closes, another one opens.

10

CLIENT MANAGEMENT

The Emperor's Old Clothes

I received a heads-up about an article from my hometown paper, provided by a family member who knew I was always interested in who was making front page news. The headline read "Judge orders family to counseling." Although it may have been the latest news to some, it was old news to me.

I first met this famous local family during my days at the newspaper. They were clients several times during my agency days for a couple of different businesses they owned. The two principal players were brothers who had a complex relationship. Many of the members of the family were a cast of characters Shakespeare or a soap opera creator could have used for inspiration.

The first time we did business with them we handled the advertising for one of their holdings: an urban shopping mall.

During the eight years we worked together they were often at odds with the merchants who leased space in their building. It was nothing new, the typical adversarial relationship of landlord and tenant. I tried to be an advocate for the tenants in order to forge a partnership between them and "the family." It was a constant struggle to be a duel agent.

The brothers were well-known for being tightfisted with their money, especially when it came to spending on advertising and promotion. I think they weren't sure if they loved it or hated it, but marketing was a snake they loved to prod. They never seemed to appreciate or understand the value of a brand and the long-term commitment required to build one. However, ironically, their behaviors branded them in a way that did not serve them or the cause. They demanded loyalty, but showed little back to others and were generally shortsighted. They never appreciated that they were in partnership with their merchants, and took them for granted. They expected everyone to invest and patiently wait for their payoff when they would not do likewise. When it came to their investments, they wanted an immediate return. This win-whatever mentality always takes its toll, and when it became clear that they would not, or could not, change, I resigned the account.

We managed to part on good terms. I moved on, or so I thought, until after a hiatus of many years and, as previously stated, the family made front page news. It was after the death of one of the brothers and the two family trees were in hot pursuit of each other, suing for power, control, and, of course, money. There was a major parting of the ways.

Knowing the family dynamic, I thought I could help. So

once again I agreed to represent them, this time for another part of their holdings: a chain of retail stores.

Of course, the best indicator of future behavior is past behavior so naturally, the problems were similar to those in the past. Frankly, what I found was no surprise. Admittedly, I am a glutton for punishment when it comes to practicing my craft. I love to help clients be more successful. I thought this could provide another opportunity to spin gold out of straw.

The initial mission now was to totally rebuild the less-than-stellar relationships they had, for a variety of reasons, with 150 of their suppliers. This was challenge enough, but there was also no appropriate budget to be able to execute an effective advertising and public relations campaign for the company either.

Can you see the shocked look on my face? Had the appropriate funds been available, we would have started promoting the company's products immediately to increase sales, but that was not possible. We had to raise money to fund the marketing campaign that we knew would turn things around and there was only one place to get the dollars we needed, and that was from the vendors.

I know it sounds crazy, but it worked like a charm.

We did a lot of listening first, and then promised the

vendors that we would create and execute a win-win advertising strategy, one that would truly benefit both sides. We would present a multi-media campaign featuring these suppliers and their products as our theme. Each product line would be presented in a way that would work in concert with their own individual brand advertising effort, and benefit them overall, beyond the increased profits they would gain through this single retail chain.

By doing this, we turned less-than-happy suppliers into contributing partners. The campaign was a complete rebuild of our client's existing image, and one that promoted the products front and center as promised. We did focus group research first, reaching out to some of the company's top shoppers, both corporate and retail customers, to get their input and to make sure we were on the same page about product mix and how the products would best be presented to them.

Whether on TV, in a catalogue, or on a billboard, the product was king. The vendors loved it, my client got lots of kudos, and the sales were good. The media partners also stepped up as usual for me, with many value-added exposures. A fine time was had by all—another win-win-win.

No matter how successful you may be, tenure is tenuous.

In the end, and after all we had done for them, and with only a few months to go to our annual contract renewal, our client said they did not need our services any longer. Not only did they not want to renew, they also did not want to fulfill their obligation to compensate us for the remaining three months of our current contract. We had been with them for many years, saved them a lot of financial grief with their vendors, but it apparently was not enough.

As with so many clients I have serviced over the years, I think they just forgot who turned on the light. They may have convinced themselves that they were the ones that did.

The reason it took several visits to the court, with many headlines documenting the to and fro of the visits, is because they obviously and consistently had a problem getting along with others, and often the situation would take the inevitable path—the parting of ways. They wanted everything from everyone immediately, but when others needed something from them, essential in aiding their cause, you had to justify it over and over. They did not practice the golden rule; they always wanted all you could give, but gave little in return. They did not give credit when it was due or show appropriate appreciation to those who deserved it. It was an overall lack of respect all around.

The judge told them to "go get counseling," but I could have saved them all that: the money, the heartache, the embarrassment and the pain. I tried to tell them that they needed to trust their partners and employees who treated their business as if it were their own. Oh yes, even their long-time employees confided to us that they too had bad feelings, but they loved what they did and needed their jobs so they just went along with it all. Their employees were afraid to tell the emperors the truth.

I tried to change them, but I could not. They would listen but never stop their shenanigans or change their ways. They acted as though they did not respect others and their expertise;

they were stingy, they were not the best partners, and they did not hold up their end of a deal. They always expected you to do more than your share.

It is a shame that people don't realize that they are the masters of their own fate if they could only see themselves for who they really are. It is always best to be open to change, practice self-reflection, and self-correct before everyone you really need abandons ship.

I lettered in two sports in high school, tennis and golf. I learned from both experiences that the best teams play well together. The best teams also have players who concentrate on their own position in order to become the best contributor to the overall goal of winning. The same is true in business.

11

FAMILY BUSINESS DYNAMICS

Who Becomes a Legend?

Have you ever known a family who is not dysfunctional in one way or the other? The problems are often magnified in business when a family attempts to make money together.

I have represented many multi-generational family businesses as clients in my time as a marketing consultant and counselor. They are difficult to manage for a variety of reasons, most of them stemming from old habits that die hard and should never have started in the first place.

One such habit inherent in all of them seems to be how the people were selected for their roles in their company. The oldest person in the family is always the President or CEO or Chairman of the Board or all three titles at once.

The oldest child is usually first in command and assumes that he or she will be catered to, regardless of whether they have the talent to deserve a title or special treatment.

Often there are other children and family members, supporting players, involved, too, such as the CEO's brother, sister, wife, or brother-in-law. Where there is one, there are usually many hands in the pot. Usually, the flock is a handful to deal with, on many essential issues, and you become an unpaid therapist in the process.

The founder of a family business brings the vision and turns an idea into reality. There is passion and drive in this act that the offspring or relatives may not be able to sustain. The generation that follows the founder may not have any passion or drive for the family business but is there none-the-less, as a favor to, or command from, the founder.

This is not helpful to any business plan.

The thing about family businesses is often that the people involved are plagued with the same basic issues that stem from the same basic characteristics and behavioral patterns. Unfortunately, sometimes passion and drive do not make the list.

For example, when one member does not value the truth, others think similarly. Or if one does not have a sense of humor that, too, may be a card missing from the deck for them all. These are factors that make communication effective, and when they are not present, relationships falter. Eventually this takes a toll on the entire operation but it definitely affects the client/agency relationship in a big way.

When problems arise, these traits and behaviors are magnified. This means that you usually have major disagreements in philosophy to deal with and this scenario demands that you have to become a therapist.

Take it from one who knows.

One gang of renown who made my client list was a multi-generational furrier who had been in business since 1895. These were the days before PETA's rise to prominence, when wearing a fur was not such an explosive issue. This was a company run by a consortium of interesting guys who were always entertaining. However, I was not surprised to see what ultimately happened to this company since I could read the writing on their walls many years ago. I knew this dynamic was combustible.

One generation was in power, two brothers who were a couple of real characters. One was always telling harmless "dirty jokes," often dressed in black slacks and a black turtleneck like an original Rat Pack devotee. His brother always dressed in a well-starched, French-cuffed, white shirt and tie. He, too, was a jokester. The two of them made me laugh with their repartee in addition to being each other's best audience. They missed their calling; they should have done standup comedy. Picture the Smother's Brothers without the singing.

The next generation involved in the company was the two sons of the elder brother. These two sons were also as different as night and day. One was soft-spoken and a real gentleman, the younger other one was aggressive and always full of his own importance, which was more annoying coming from someone so green. Like their father and uncle before them, they were very different in style. The younger one dressed like his father in the crisp shirt with glistening cufflinks. He was a chip off the old block. The eldest was a gentle sprit, smart and soft-spoken. He often had a hard time getting a word in edgewise.

It was clear to me that the younger son was going to bulldoze his way into power at some point in the future and I knew if he did he would mess up the whole applecart. Many years later that is exactly what happened. He got into a battle royal with PETA demonstrators, and apparently did not know how to handle the situation in a constructive way. The city government tried to step in to mediate but the protesters were persistent outside their store. Even though there were others selling furs in the marketplace, they did not become the target like this company did and hence, did not suffer like this company did. Unfortunately, it was their ultimate demise.

So after over 100 years in business, the company closed its doors, all on the watch of one overconfident hothead. He was over his pay grade doing any type of marketing for the company to begin with, even back when I was involved with them many years before this cataclysmic end. He obviously did not know how to handle public relations in the midst of a major fashion and social cultural issue. They needed a bonafide professional to help, but this guy never thought he really needed any outside counsel. One person who did not understand what business he was in was responsible for taking the company down. He should have hired an expert but thought he knew best.

If only they had listened to those who knew better how to handle these types of situations, they might have ended up on a different path.

When they were my client, they were hard to convince because even though they went along with our suggestions, they never really believed in anything other than their own opinions. They had no basis for forming some of the opinions they held with fervor, especially when it came to marketing. But that did not stop them. They felt empowered by the safety of other members of their family who thought similarly. I think they got little or no pushback because, deep down, they all shared common beliefs.

There are a few other family business dynasties I have worked with over the years, and some of those experiences were different. These other companies survived due to a couple of different factors—such as no direct competition—but mostly because they recognized the necessity to have outside expertise on their corporate team. This was also because they trusted us and allowed us to function.

Family businesses operate with ideas that are long-held and often shared. The apple does not fall far from the tree.

12

TARGETING

K.I.S.S. and Sell

Another multi-generational family business I represented was an umbrella company. They also manufacture and sell other products, too, such as hats and outerwear, because rainwear is their beat. They understood how to create a great product line, and I understood how to harness the power of media to reach their targets. This was a good partnership while it lasted which it did for over 10 years.

We were instrumental in a number of projects for this company including the creation of a television spot, shot one hot August night in 85-degree weather. This was ironic because the city where we created the commercial is well known for its regular and persistent rainfall, and is rarely hot in the late evening, even in summer. As a result, we had to bring in rain machines to create the effect we were looking for, a normal, regular old rainy day in town.

Besides executing television advertising, we did packaging and public relations for this company, and in each case it was always a very lengthy process. Although they were a retail manufacturer, they also thought that this experience qualified them to be advertising experts. Like the movie *Groundhog Day,* this story is repetitive: same story, different client.

Like so many before them, convincing this company to use TV advertising took time, but once they had their commercial "in the can," they liked it so much that they wanted it to be seen. They presented it to their top customers, major department store chains, offering it as a co-op opportunity. This meant they would share in the cost of airing the commercial and would tag the spot with the store's logo. This was done with several big retailers in large markets across the USA. It was another example of a win-win arrangement.

I had done a good job of selling the president on the benefits of TV advertising, and so he assumed that I would want to use TV for most projects. To their surprise I did not, and the reason was clear. It is not always necessary to use the broad reach of television when the mission is to reach only a designated few.

Identifying the correct target audience is always the first step in developing a successful marketing strategy.

Because I always begin with the end in mind, in this case, there were only a couple of people we needed to reach, preferably in a big and meaningful way. The message this company wanted to communicate to this small group was that they valued their relationship and wanted it to continue. The people they wanted to reach happened to be the CEO, the divisional merchandise manager, and the accessory buyer for a large well-known fashion store chain they did business with for years.

This company wanted to protect their vital, existing vendor relationship with this fashion chain while at the same time expanding their business selling a different line of products to discount chains. There was also increasing competition so they also wanted to appear as a leader and as the most important vendor in the category.

I introduced them to the wonderful power of outdoor advertising.

In the spirit of the season, the holiday period was also the perfect time for a free gift. Every retailer likes to dominate the market during this most important time, and what company doesn't like additional free exposure? This scenario was tailor-made for outdoor.

The gift bestowed was a huge wallscape: a large piece of art painted on the facade of a building displaying a beautifully designed umbrella with the fashion store's logo prominent. This turned out to be viewed as a huge Christmas card to this retailer, courtesy of my client, placed right across the street—and easily seen—from the large plate glass window of the CEO's condo. It was also in the line of sight of the rest of the targeted group of merchandisers as they walked to their offices located in the flagship store. I did a little research to determine their path from a parking lot they used a block away. Of course, customers saw it, too, walking or driving by, and that turned into increased sales as a bonus. It was two mints in one.

As the mural was being painted onto the wall, the picture was revealed from top to bottom. At the top was the retailer's logo, then the bold patterned umbrella with my client's logo at the bottom. The wallscape was only partially done, but it was clear what was being shown and by whom, when the CEO of the store called my client to thank him for his wonderful "holiday greeting." Clearly, it made a big impression and immediately distinguished my client as a valuable vendor.

The wallscape was the gift that kept on giving, throughout the holiday season and beyond, courtesy of one of my best partners, the outdoor company, who gave us more than we paid for. They gave us many extra gratis months of exposure until they sold the space to the next advertiser. It was the fastest return on investment from a media purchase I ever witnessed.

It also proved to me what I always knew. There's no need to make it complicated or expensive when simple does the trick.

13

STANDING OUT

Feed Them and Reap

I have served a lot of family businesses in my time, as I have already explained, and their dynamics are always learning opportunities. I have worked with multi-generational dynasties and sibling duets. Another example of a client I served was run by a couple of brothers who started a shoe company after coming to America and finding no clogs like those found everywhere in their native Denmark.

Although the vast majority of my clients rarely knew anything about advertising, most of them did know that the best way to get attention for their brand or company was to stand apart from their competition. All successful brands know their "unique selling proposition" or USP.

Great products and services stand out from their competition in many ways. However, when a company just follows the leader in their category, lemming-like as most businesses do, there is no USP. Rather, there is just a different version of the same thing, a different rendition of the same song. To be similar requires no risk taking or leadership and so there is often no corresponding big payoff either.

I learned long ago that rarity equals value.

This was not the case with this shoe company who was our client for many years. They knew about unique selling and would demonstrate this in a number of ways to their customers, vendors, and staff. They were masters at relationship building that was always a great USP for them.

During market weeks, beyond their creative product offerings, they would use food and atmosphere to stand out from the many other shoe company presentations going on simultaneously. All the largest and most successful shoe companies, like many other industry groups, present their product lines in showrooms during these market weeks, all hoping for orders for the upcoming fashion season. The mission was to get orders and hope the goods would sell through, insuring more business going forward.

This company knew that there was only one opportunity to make a first impression and, if done well, that it can be a lasting one.

So every day during the major footwear market shows they would present their line in their showroom alongside the most amazing Danish smorgasbord buffet. This was straight from their heritage but it was also straight to the heart and stomachs of the merchandisers attending the show. All the major players from the most important retail chains and independent shoe stores alike would show up for lunch like clockwork. Their food presentation was legendary.

Of course, that was not the only way they stood out.

The creative director of this company was also a standout, and one of their significant points of difference. Berna was, and still is, an industry leader. She was never a follower; she walked to a beat of her own natural creative instincts. With incredible energy, ability and style she helped the brothers build a successful company with multiple brands. She, too, was part of their USP.

Our connection to Berna dated back to the fashion office in the department store where I first cut my teeth in the promotion business many years before. She was hired to take over the post of corporate fashion director when my agency partner retired. After some time, she left to join this shoe company.

We had a shared history with her, and when the time came that this shoe company needed to create a national fashion advertising campaign, she came calling. She knew who to trust to deliver for her and her company when it counted. All good relationships have trust at their foundation and that foundation is based on two key components: character and competence. We fit that bill.

It was the week before Christmas and everyone in our company just wanted to break free for a needed time-out. However, opportunity knocked, and we answered the call. The request was for us to design a magazine ad featuring one of the company's hot new silhouettes. They needed it fast—in just a couple of weeks—in order to meet the advertising deadline of the national fashion magazine where they wanted it to appear.

We created the ad; the first of many we would execute for them over 10 years during this long-lasting partnership. Overall, this was one of the most profitable and challenging client relationships we would ever have, and we loved every minute of it.

I made friends with the sales managers and publishers of the fashion magazines in much the same way I did with those in broadcast and outdoor media, and the results were exactly the same. My USP: I treated them differently and consequently I received different treatment from them in return. In this case it resulted in better placement than our spending should have earned. My clients' ads were always in a great spot in the magazine, often up front among other companies who bought significantly more pages a year than I did for this company. I was a very small fish in a very large pond but my clients were treated like whales.

Once again my theory proved correct: People give money to people they like and in this case, money meant location, location, location.

We had many memorable occasions with this company that included an invitation to join their sales team for a company-wide meeting in Hong Kong. During this event, they pulled out all the stops and it was a very exciting and educational trip as we saw all the aspects of shoe manufacturing up close and personal. It was a once-in a-lifetime experience.

This shoe company was like us: different in several ways from the others in their line of business, including how they liked to operate. They treated their sales force like partners and did many special things for them to prove it, and in my opinion, the company blossomed as a result.

Although the co-owners were often mistrusting of the effectiveness of advertising overall, always weighing the benefits of doing it, they did trust their creative director, she trusted us, and the company ultimately benefitted.

The two most important active ingredients in business are respect and trust, and when these two elements are in play, magic happens. In this case, the magic was also served up with a luscious Danish smorgasbord buffet.

14

TEAM BUILDING

Rumpelstiltskin

You remember the old fairy tale about Rumpelstiltskin? It's where the girl spins gold out of straw. I think that is how the story goes but for sure, this completely fits as a description of my personal story working with a group of art schools.

It was not the first time I was living this fairy tale in real life. I had been there and done this before. This time the client was a network of colleges I served in a number of different locations, campuses in cities across the US and Canada, including one in my home base.

They were a very successful company in those days, despite some of their advertising campaigns, often painfully outdated in approach. I don't think they had changed their basic creative direction since their inception, other than a few, slight adjustments over the years. It was not a case of "don't fix what is not broken" either, because the effectiveness of their advertising was always a bone of contention. This was even the case with their enrolled students who thought the advertising was surprisingly bad. I heard this repeatedly while conducting student focus group research for the company.

This was not my first rodeo with proprietary schools, so I did have some history to draw from to help them climb out from under that rock. As usual, advertising was always under the microscope and being questioned by corporate. Apparently, they never reached out for opinions from the right people. They fell in love with their own creative direction, regardless of how their target audience felt and because of this mindset, their visual message was always weak.

However, all that said, and like so many other schools, this did not stop them from attempting to make a science out of the results by carefully tracking each and every potential student to see how and why they came to contact the college initially. Of course, this methodology was not reliable because I had long ago learned that people seldom remember where they heard about anything. There are often many reasons why people reach out to a business or purchase something.

The fact that their advertising was seen as so passé was surprising since this was a company issuing Bachelor's degrees in the arts: graphic design, web design, video production, photography, culinary arts, to name a few of their program offerings. This should have helped them deliver a more creative approach to their advertising effort and an appreciation for one that was more cutting-edge.

I first became involved with the company at one of the most

successful campuses in the chain. This was due to one of their senior executives who brought us on board. Doug is a guy who knows what business he is in, and he knew he needed some help. He is an expert in admissions management and had been a partner with us before during the years when we represented another school chain. We had a long history of partnership and trust between us and it continues to this day.

Our business relationship started anew because Doug, unlike some others in that company, wanted to try to find answers to some of his marketing questions from current students in order to create the right message and tone for marketing support materials going forward. I conducted some focus group research at the school. The students who participated were from all levels and programs, an exciting cultural mix of people, and they were very expressive. They were clearly enrolled in this college for a reason. As I suspected, by asking the right questions, I was told everything we needed to know.

As the focus groups evolved, and based on the thoughtful and excellent commentaries emanating from these students, I thought it was striking that a simple testimonial TV campaign had not been produced to date.

This is my stock in trade— testimonial advertising—and I have created many different types of testimonial campaigns for my clients over the years, using their customers as the on-air talent.

This is because I have a natural curiosity about what makes people tick and I can usually get them to tell me everything I need to know once we start talking.

I can also read faces. I do not ask stupid questions and I play off what I see in their body language as they express their true feelings.

I understand and accept that 90% of all communication is nonverbal.

At the time, the commercials that were airing for this school were more than stale and, as I said, not reflective of the creativity of the curriculum or campus experience. They were tired old reruns, the same commercials they had been running for years, and similar to all the other commercials in the school universe.

So the challenge was to rebuild an outdated broadcast image and brand identity with no officially ordained budget to do so. It also had to be executed under the corporate radar. This was not a problem for me, because we had done creative rebirth before but doing so under the radar of a corporate advertising department was a new spin.

The creative content for this college on TV was remedied quickly, thanks to the focus group participants. I picked out the students I felt had the most ability to communicate effectively on camera and interviewed them on tape. I posed questions centered on creativity and what it meant to them. We had a conversation on camera, and then I edited their stories to 30 seconds. The production team consisted of me and one of the college's video production instructors with a camera and a wireless microphone. We shot the commercials in the school halls or classrooms. Final editing was done in the school production lab, after hours, when the students were gone.

For no outside production expense we produced a very memorable television campaign. A billboard campaign was also created from stills taken by one of the school's photography students who was present during the filming of the commercials. The outdoor campaign was launched simultaneously with the debut of the new TV spots that gave even more visibility to the brand. More on the outdoor effort I spearheaded in a minute.

The college received written accolades from their competition in the market—the state university across town—who said the campaign was "refreshing and finally and actually demonstrating what the school was capable of." Another note came from one of the sales executives from one of the network affiliated TV stations in town who said he "had been following them for years" and was happy to see they had finally turned over a new leaf with a campaign that "was leaps and bounds over those in the past." He was not someone I knew or did business with directly either.

I was very proud of the campaign I created because I was able to see a great new and improved image come to life with little to no intervention. That was a rare occurrence. This was my one-woman show moment, and needless to say, the whole process was very gratifying. The campaign had a long life on the air.

Because I had a great relationship with the largest outdoor media company, as I did with the broadcasters, I was asked to step in to try to secure billboard locations by their corporate media director after the TV campaign came out from the shadows and was running. This long-term professional planner and buyer had worked for major advertising companies in her career and yet she was unable to secure any locations in this market. She was told there was nothing available, but that was not the case when I contacted them. Not only did I get great locations but I also received gratis space, too. The college continued to use billboards for many years forward and they increased their brand awareness as a result.

The bottom line was the whole campaign increased enrollments. I was elated and gratified on many levels.

As a result of securing the billboard locations, and after this media queen and I had become partners in crime, I was asked to help her better orchestrate their annual TV buy. I was asked to help her to be more effective. As I said, she had large New York City agency experience and so she did things in a very traditional way and completely different from my approach. We got along well and she was more than happy to have me as a partner. It was another win-win relationship. I made her look good, we had fun, and I made a few bucks in the process as a consultant.

The stations loved it the most. Unlike in the past, I told them up front what the annual commitment would be so they were not in the dark about what they would be realizing. Because I negotiated the buy based on annual spending, that meant they were not having to resell their viability and programming over and over again. Because I did not rely on ratings to decide what programming was a good fit, my sales reps saved hours of time and effort, proving what was already obvious to me. That dance was never part of my demands from the media. Some stations also got quite a bit more than they were used to as well.

In return, and as usual, I got a bundle of extras for my client. I received many "gifts with purchase" for a number of reasons. They knew what to expect and they were treated with respect. They were my partners, not just vendors, and I treated them as such. I cut out all the needless and redundant paperwork and haggling typically a part of media buying. I never questioned the rates but told them I expected to be treated fairly and they always delivered to my expectation. It is easy to find out what others are paying for programming so I was no patsy and they knew it. The respect was a two-way street and the result was a win all around for the stations, for my client, and for my company.

I was like a magician turning focus groups into better TV commercials and an outdoor campaign to boot. I delivered more TV and outdoor exposure to the college without spending one more cent and better than my client had tried to do before and could not.

The magic show is actually very easy to perform. It just comes down to one thing: People give money to people they like.

15

PARTNERSHIPS

What's in a Name?

My marketing magic show continued when I was asked to assist another art college within the same school network that I had worked with before. This time it was because the company had acquired another school in a new market for the chain that happened to be my hometown.

The job required a different strategy from day one because we were starting from scratch. There was very little advertising budget to work with and little to zero name recognition either. To make matters worse, there wasn't even a sign on the building.

The school had a history as a fashion institute, a college teaching fashion merchandising and apparel design. It had been run by a local, well-established husband and wife team. They had owned the school for a very long time and their name was on the door. They were the legendary big fish in the town's small fashion pond and they had little to no direct competition. It was a niche business and accordingly, their census was always small.

After many years, the couple wanted to sell the school and retire, so it was acquired by my client, a nationwide degree granting art school chain. The acquiring company had a good reputation and awareness in the many markets where they did business however; contrary to their internally held belief, the company name had no recognized brand identity in this market. Miles away on the other side of the country at their corporate headquarters, they thought they were a household name largely because they had another campus 160 miles away. In truth, they had no clue how little their name resonated in their new neck of the woods.

This may be why this company was slow to put up a sign on the building. They mistakenly thought that as soon as word of mouth spread and people found out they had come to town the phone would start ringing. However, when they did finally put the new name of the school up on the building, the sign was temporary, a flimsy piece of plastic that quickly got torn in the wind. It was left like this for months too until it finally came down completely.

In retrospect, it was probably for the best that it came down because the building was shopworn and badly in need of repair and updating. Since the company had no intention of staying in this location beyond the current lease expiration, there was no effort to make changes in the short term. Eventually the school moved into much better digs in the hippest part of town, but that was 18 months later.

Even though they had Kelly at the helm, one of the best admissions managers in the business, their expectations did not match the reality of the situation. They were located in a poor facility, with no name awareness, and no appropriate dollars allotted to introduce their name and offerings to the community.

Promoting a company with such poor marketing basics is akin to building a house on a cracked foundation. It was even more problematic since this company should have known better as experts in the creative arts, teaching industrial and interior design.

I had a challenge before me that I took on with gusto as usual. I pulled out my old bag of reliable tricks, using the same time-tested strategies of thinking out of the box and establishing effective win-win partnerships.

With the help of three media entities, I created and executed a couple of significant special events that gave the college prominence and press. The events were consistent with the school's mission and gained the attention of their target markets: current students, prospective students, parents, teachers, high school counselors, and employers. I also wanted to reach their current staff and faculty to make them feel proud when they saw their college promoted in the community.

The first event was dubbed the "Creative Career Symposium." It was co-sponsored by one of the local TV affiliates and it took place in their studios on a Saturday. There were two sessions, morning and afternoon. We reached out to the school's advisory boards and our other creative contacts to bring together some of the best creative minds from the community to be on a panel. The speakers were all experts in their respective fields, aligned with the program offerings of the college. The panel included an award-winning cinematographer, a very prominent worldwide ad agency creative director, an independent apparel designer, a successful interior decorator, a well-known special effects video producer, and a top graphic designer. It was a stellar group.

Our TV co-sponsor extensively promoted this event in all their best programming and they also produced the public service commercial gratis, all because this was a fundraiser for the state's Art Educators Association. The value received for just the on-air portion of the promotion alone far exceeded the client's actual annual TV spending with this station at that time. They knew it would come back to them over the long haul with me in charge and, of course, it did.

The interactive symposium was well attended by an enthusiastic mix of our target audiences—prospective students interested in the arts and their parents, local area art teachers and counselors. Of course, the admissions representatives from the college were in attendance, too, and they were able to invite many of the attendees to the school's next open house, scheduled on the following weekend. Naturally, that was no coincidence but part of the plan to help insure a crowd for this important marketing activity.

The "Creative Career Symposium" was a major success for all involved and became an annual event, repeated for many years. It directly supported the network of high school art teachers and counselors who would now be more aware of this college and more likely to refer students for their post-secondary art education as a result.

The second promotional event was in tandem with the Comedy Central network, thanks to a partnership I struck with the local cable company. Cable advertising was in its infancy in those days and was struggling to gain respectability with the TV media buyers. As I said before, most media buyers are followers waiting for ratings and then paying more for advertising time as a result.

In exchange for a respectable percentage of our small TV budget, the cable company stepped up and with the dedication of their promotion director, Jamie, delivered a live comedy event that the school co-sponsored. Again, as with the Symposium, the proceeds of the ticket sales for the "Make Me Laugh" live comedy show event went to support the Art Educators Association.

I also reached out to my other partner, the largest outdoor media company, and negotiated for free billboards to promote both events because they were both charity fundraisers. Of course, it also mattered that I had been a friend and major supporter, purchasing lots of billboards and wallscapes for many years, for many clients, in several markets from this company. This outdoor company, like the TV station and the cable company, knew that I would eventually direct an increasing number of dollars to them.

That is exactly how it played out. This college became a consistent advertiser in short order and continued to do outdoor for many, many, years. The outdoor advertising I executed for this school brought other educational clients to outdoor advertising as well, much like what happened with my TV campaigns. Someone had to show the rest of them the better way.

I executed many outdoor campaigns for this company's campuses in a variety of different markets from coast to coast, in the US and Canada, from Vancouver, BC to Toronto, from Seattle to New York City and several markets in between.

I generally purchase a few large bulletins at a time, with rotating locations every month. Picking the right locations with a great rotation strategy is the key. This is more economical and helps a budget go further. Everyone sees the message over time without the creative becoming wallpaper that is eventually ignored due to too much familiarity and oversaturation. Less is definitely more.

Sometimes it has nothing to do with how much money you have to spend, but rather the ability to think outside the box.

Overall there was a large promotional effort for very little out-of-pocket expense in the beginning when the budget was slim and our client's needs were big. Between the two events, we raised more money for the state's Art Educators Association than they had in their original annual budget. The money went directly into the classrooms of high school art programs throughout the state so you can imagine how that played with those targeted teachers.

Most important is the ability to team up with the right partners that always pays off with major results. Business is, and has always been, all about relationship building. Good partnerships pay big dividends in the long term.

16

GETTING ATTENTION

Give and Ye Shall Receive

As I have already demonstrated with several examples, one thing that always makes a big impression wherever you go is a free gift. It is amazing that no matter what your financial position may or may not be, or how much money and stuff you may possess, getting something for free is so satisfying.

Free gifts come in many forms but are always noticed and appreciated. They can be food samples in a grocery store, cute little soaps and toiletries in a hotel bathroom, party favors, perfume samples in the department store, or hot bread brought to your table in a restaurant as you read the menu.

Gifts always make a statement, but sometimes they can also get you publicity.

Once upon a time, two former colleagues from my department store days came calling in need. They had both been a buyer and divisional merchandise manager for the store where I cut my marketing teeth, and had subsequently gone on to larger and larger posts to include positions as chief executives for another well-known national retailer. Together they rebuilt that company during their tenure as top decision makers and eventually orchestrated the selling of that company. They made lots of money in that deal and deserved that result.

After that, they did their homework to determine what their next challenge would be. They landed their sights on the cosmetic industry, which was in flux at the time because smaller, cosmetic-only chains had come on the scene and were taking business away from the traditional department stores. This was their new frontier, and based on their joint expertise they birthed a new company selling a line of interlocking beauty and skin care products sold under a single banner that could be used by everyone on earth. The organic products had no excess packaging and were not tested on animals. These were two key points of difference in the category.

They initially called us because they needed to find a competent store manager for one of their first stores where my agency was located, and they hoped we could deliver someone to fit the bill. We had similar ideas about competency and of course, we directed them to a great candidate whom they hired. Then they opened two more stores with coast-to-coast expansion plans.

On the heels of delivering that personnel favor, we got hired to be their quasi ad agency of record but once again, as with so many clients I had over the years, there was no traditional advertising budget or plan for one. There was an elaborate merchandising plan though, with dollars slated for signage and targeted direct mail. They wanted us to handle this sales support creative, and we agreed to do it. This turned out to be an extremely stressful engagement because they were often unwilling to let go of their grip on anything that was considered the creative process to allow the most effective result to bloom. I'm all for team play but everyone needs to play a different instrument.

Creative by committee is not the way to get the best results.

Providing their creative turned out to be a lost leader for us, but it did lead to a more profitable and fun public relations program that we executed for them. The goal was to get publicity for this three-store-but-growing regional chain on a national stage to impact investors, real estate developers, and of course, retail sales. They wanted to impress investors to help influence the flow of capital they needed to grow the business. They wanted to impress developers so they would be offered and then be able to secure the lucrative prime spaces they wanted in the best and largest malls in the country, preferably right next to the best and most successful fashion retail anchor tenants. Naturally, they also wanted to drive traffic into their stores and thus increase revenue.

When the CEO asked me if I could get them the publicity they coveted, I quickly told him the truth. I said that I had no experience in generating public relations on this scale, but he insisted that I would be the best one to do it. This was the one and only time that he showed confidence in my expertise and it was when I thought I had none to offer. They were finally willing to let go of something.

So with the aid of our office manager and general assistant of everything going on at our company, we parlayed my existing relationships with national magazine sales associates—ones I knew from buying space and others I knew who had pitched their publications to me—to reach out to all the beauty editors of all the top relevant magazines in the country. Over a relatively short period of time, during a series of visits to New York and Los Angeles, my partner and I schlepped our client's products served up as "gifts" to all those who could be influenced. Our mission was to get those products featured on their magazine pages as soon as possible, and we achieved great results.

Because we had a variety of clients, I had a great network of media reps to draw from and they got me to the right people. We talked our way into appointments. This was a royal schmooze fest, executed by me and my right-hand office manager, Susie. This was just one example of her many abilities. To best illustrate her contributions and talents over 14 years, I repeatedly told her that she could not quit or retire before I did.

Once we were in front of the beauty editors, it was clear that the "gifts" we brought for them closed the deal and ultimately got us the coverage we wanted. We came in with cute shopping bags, loaded to the brim. We brought demonstration products, too, so the editor had a bag full of fresh goodies for her personal use.

This was also about timing as it turned out, because often

the magazines would be close to deadline and an art director was madly searching for a last-minute product or story to complete a page layout. The products we brought to their attention were often just what they needed at the time, and they were right there ready for their close-up. There was no time wasted waiting for a product to be shipped or delivered to them to get it photographed. Like I said before, everyone loves a free gift.

The results of our efforts speak for themselves: 44 editorial exposures in 23 different national publications in 20 consecutive months. From *Vogue* to *GQ*, from *Parents* to *Cosmopolitan*, my client got more than they paid for, and my partner and I had some great times in Manhattan and LA as a fringe benefit.

A win-win-win on this one for the client, for the magazine and for our agency.

The best return on this client's publicity investment was achieved as a result of the conversation I had with one of the New York based editors. Since this is a very well-known, national magazine I was asked where the stores were located in reference to the availability of the products, should a story be printed in the magazine. I was asked if they had a store in New York City, and the answer was no. I was asked if they had stores on the East Coast, and I said "no." Finally she said, "Are there any stores east of the Mississippi?" Again, I said "no."

I still remember the look on that editor's face that told me she was conflicted. She really enjoyed the gift of the "best hand cream she had ever used" still fresh on her fingertips, but she was trying to justify if she could give publicity to this company and product line based on my client's current store footprint. She asked, "How would our readers get these products?" Without missing a beat, I told her that her readers could order by phone now by calling their 800 number. This was before websites were common practice. I then said, "You will see, soon this company will be the GAP of cosmetics."

I could see her mood ring changing.

The company was mentioned in one of the items on their "Beauty Flash" page—the start of their editorial section quoting my one-liner, "The GAP of cosmetics" along with the 800 number. The calls came in like gangbusters. This was the first editorial mention we received and because the 800 number was one of the phone lines into their corporate office, the results were recognized immediately.

With this one piece of publicity the company launched their direct response division, the only part of the company that survives today.

Despite their vast retail expertise and great product line, the reason I think they had to close their store chain was because they never seemed to fully appreciate or recognize their partners' abilities and contributions. They were not loyal. After all we did for them in their formative years with this company, when they had grown from one to 60 stores, they thought they needed a new light bulb. They never seemed to understand what they had with us, and we were burning bright for them.

They interviewed many larger, well-established agencies and signed a deal with one of them, bidding us adieu in the process.

No sooner had we been replaced when we got a call from

their new account executive at the new agency of record. He wanted to know our history because he was unsure of how to move forward with his new client. He had no idea what to do and was frustrated already, for many of the same reasons we had been before him. They had no reasonable budget to work with, and he was used to big budgets. It's easy when you have lots of money to spend because you can do everything, and cover all the bases. He was used to not having to take much risk. He also was realizing that there was no commitment to marketing the brand institutionally, as he was accustomed to with his other accounts. He was not like us either, because he was used to being a big fish in a big pond with lots of layers of support. Welcome to our world.

Turns out they apparently had no intention of staying with that larger agency because in short order they convinced this account executive to jump ship and join the company as their employee. They stole him away from his agency and thought they could do it all in-house. In the end, the bigger agency they hired did next to nothing for them, and they lost an account executive in the mix.

It was not long thereafter that the company was forced into bankruptcy and closed all their stores. We received a legal notification because we had been a supplier, but since we had been paid in full, there was nothing that required our time or attention at the court hearing. It was sad because there was so much promise and success and the outcome could have been different if they only had known what business THEY were in.

In the end and in retrospect, we actually got out while the getting was good, but I again was reminded that in the advertising business one should never interpret success as security.

17

CREATING TRAFFIC

Let Them Eat Truffles

When one door closes another one opens and this once again proved to be the case when we got a call from one of the former executives from our former client, the cosmetics company.

Paul was reaching out to us because he knew what we could do; he had benefited from our work first-hand. He appreciated our publicity efforts and results because it was his responsibility to acquire and negotiate all the real estate deals for the 500+ skin and body care retail stores they eventually opened. Our publicity campaign helped him sell the viability of the company when they had little to no history of performance as a retail chain.

Paul had moved on, too, and at this time he was working for a very famous mail order food, home, and garden company that was expanding. They had brought together some veteran retail minds to execute the rollout of a coast-to-coast store chain. The plan was to locate these stores in outlet malls, at this time a newly expanding retail concept, and our marketing expertise was called on to help them achieve their corporate objectives.

Since this was a retail food company, they were already big into sampling and knew its power. They used it very effectively in their long-standing flagship store which was located close to their corporate headquarters. They had every intention of going full steam ahead with it in these outlet stores as well.

Of course, there was no real budget earmarked for advertising these grand openings. Why would they need advertising? Like so many of my clients, this company believed they were a household name, and once their customers saw their name on a sign they would march right in. They also believed that since they were going to be situated in a great location in these centers, putting their stores in the best of these malls, they thought great traffic was essentially guaranteed and would lead to great sales as a result.

Well, what else is NOT new?

My clients often thought they didn't have to advertise because they believed that traffic equaled sales. Unfortunately, it's just not that easy.

With this client it was a given that they would have a budget for "sampling," so I thought why fight city hall? We just elaborated on their sampling effort to reach out to their target customer, the chief shopper. Our plan was to drive women into our client's new stores using two of their private label products as bait: coffee and truffles.

Coffee was an easy selection out of a store full of choices because it is simple to dispense and often habitual. If someone gets hooked on a certain brand of coffee, they will most likely stick with it and come back repeatedly to buy it.

Truffles are generally hard to resist. Even on a diet, women will make an exception when really good chocolate is involved, especially when it's free. It's only a wee bit after all, so how many calories could it possibly be?

With these two tasty and irresistible "gifts" to give away, we developed a two-pronged strategy.

To coincide with each store's grand opening day, we sent gift baskets full of coffee and truffles, plus a few other items to properly represent the company's overall merchandise mix, to the top five radio stations who best reached women in every market of each new store. We sent these treat collections to the attention of the on-air staff, and timed their arrival to the start of the important morning drive and mid-day time slots in hopes of receiving on-air chatter in order to reach the greatest number of potential customers.

The on-air personalities loved getting these gift baskets and wasted no time eating them while commenting about them on the air. We included a press release about the store opening in their area and its location, so they carried on about the company as we had hoped they would do. This was the valuable publicity we needed and all for the cost of a few products, funded by the sampling budget.

We also wanted to create a handout, so we tapped into the "sales support materials" budget to fund that part of the plan.

This was another source for dollars in their approved budget, which covered the creation of all their printed promotional materials. Since they did not consider sales support as "advertising," they always had monies available here. It was a game I knew how to play from many years digging for dollars in corporate budgets in order to create something needed from no directly allocated funds.

With this found money we created a cute, little card die-cut in the shape of a coffee cup with a truffle by its side. The cards were perforated in a way that enabled us to secure a count of who took us up on the offer for coffee, the truffle, or both.

We orchestrated the distribution of these "coupons" to all adult women in the parking lots of each mall during the first three days of each store's grand opening week. We approached our target females as they got out of their cars, greeting them with our free offer for a double jolt of pleasure. Of course, they did not resist and came right in.

In each community we also worked with a local talent agency and negotiated with them to get our cards handed out gratis by young actors looking for a legitimate gig to put on their resume. Because this company was very well-known as a purveyor of fruit products and preserves, we used available company costumes, dressing up

"The Fruit Kids"

these actors as colorful pieces of fruit. They looked absolutely adorable and were disarming to everyone they approached. It was another win-win, for our client and for the actors.

Overall, and in every case, each store enjoyed increased traffic and sales, not just in coffee and chocolate because once in the stores, the women were attracted to the full product mix. As I know first-hand as a chief shopper myself, just because I may go into a store for one thing, I often end up buying something that I had no intention of buying because I did not know it existed, and/or that I just had to have it. This is why we targeted our message to the chief shopper and did so with the irresistible free gifts of caffeine and chocolate.

We just made her an offer she could not refuse.

18

SALES SUPPORT

Beefcake and Raspberries

Making an offer that cannot be refused is what a marketing mission is based on. It is the simple way to make a sale, so this was again the strategy I employed for two other clients.

The first of these was the only Mercedes-Benz dealer in the region. At the time we were representing them they had to accept that, due to their successful history, the region had the largest market share of this brand of vehicles per capita in the nation. This family-owned dealership had enjoyed many years of prosperity, and they saw no reason that it could not continue. This meant they had to sell more cars to a market already well saturated with their brand.

The other client was a food processor who had developed a special method of "flash freezing" their locally grown berries, fruits, and veggies. In addition to packaging these products under their own label, they also sold their produce to other companies for "private label." Our mission here was to help them break into the retail marketplace with their own brand in key markets with major grocery chains.

In both cases, our goal was to create incentives to get our clients' products and services noticed and by doing so get tangible results.

The Mercedes-Benz company has great branding and at that time, they had produced a beautiful brochure of the model our client wanted to promote. This piece was designed to look like a coffee table book in quality and heft rather than your typical brochure, and when I saw it I knew that we could use it to our advantage for little to no cost. Companies often have access to branded marketing materials from their vendors and so we quickly placed an order for as many of these books as they would give us.

I researched the dealer's customer database, looking at their past purchasers. I decided that the best way to approach the challenge was to reach out to the CEOs at the top companies in the region. We knew they would or could be interested so we used this free brochure as one of our hooks.

Again, working with a local talent agency, we hired a group of tall, dark, and handsome young men—actors and models—dressed them in tuxedos, top hats and tails and sent them out to deliver the books to these company top executives. The brochure was placed in a gorgeous black and white gift-wrapped package fastened with a large red bow. We did this knowing that most of these executives had female assistants and we also knew, as women ourselves, that they would take notice of a gorgeous man dressed to the nines bearing a beautifully wrapped gift. How many women could resist? Very few. How many of these women would help ensure that the package got opened as soon as possible? The vast majority.

The "gifts" got delivered and as the booklets were being perused, a supporting radio campaign ran on all the stations catering to the business community. The commercial was simple and low-key, just the owner of the dealership speaking directly to his customers, explaining why he loved to sell this brand of vehicles.

The result was that this company sold more cars. Mission accomplished once again.

The food processor's story posed the opposite challenge. The company had no brand awareness with the retailers they wanted to do business with going forward because their business had been largely private label. They wanted to get their product line into the freezer cases of the major grocery store chains in one of the largest markets in the country, far away from their fields. We would need to create something to excite store managers while also getting the necessary nod of approval from these stores' top decision makers who ultimately had the final say on shelf or freezer case space despite no retail sales history.

Once again, understanding the target audience is essential and when it comes to the grocery store, and almost any store for that matter, the target is female, and so for me it was easy to figure out what would make an effective introduction and impression.

To tell this story we combined two tactics that work well

to deliver results with this group, television and recipes. This was way before Food Network, *Rachel Ray* or any of the myriad cooking shows now on the air.

We produced a video about the company and its products and presented it in a specially designed cabinet that could be rolled into a store, fitting nicely at the end of a frozen fruit aisle. The cabinet also had a built-in recipe card rack filled with recipe cards featuring and centered on the products. The video showed where the produce originated and how it was flash frozen in addition to demonstrating different dishes prepared on camera. The recipes cards were available as takeaways, and the takeaway here is the company got the results it was after.

People are moved by a story. If the story behind the product is compelling, the product is more revered and valued.

Stories sell and can change hearts and minds if presented with enough emotional power.

In both campaigns, we made a definite splash with our efforts and that rippled into sales. It is a simple formula: Know your target and think outside the box.

19

Multi-Level Marketing

"a day at the mall"©

My extensive history and experience in retail marketing have afforded me many opportunities and I have gained insight from them all. After the many different challenges with independent stores, regional and national chains, and retail manufacturers, I suppose it was inevitable and predictable that I would eventually end up representing shopping malls.

Retail was always a perfect fit for me.

I love to shop. I love the experience and the thrill of the chase. I love to find a bargain when I least expect it. I love to buy presents and actually prefer shopping for others more than myself because others are easier to please. Mostly, the joy of giving turns me on. Overall, I fully understand the shopper mentality from a personal perspective, based on a lifetime of doing so.

However, when I first got involved with shopping malls I had no idea how they functioned from a marketing perspective, how they were structured and why, even though I had represented stores in many different malls for many years. Up until that time I was always on the store side of the equation.

After working as the agency of record at several super-regional malls, I came to understand more about the real challenge of promoting them. Actually, they are just big plots of real estate, often part of the portfolios of large-scale investment groups such as teachers' unions. The investors, their fund managers, and the real estate management firms involved in their day-to-day operations seemed to me to have little to no significant experience in retail. They also did not seem to demonstrate proper respect for those who did. They seemed to treat the mall as if it were just a large parking lot, focusing on security and traffic patterns more than the softer side of retail business. They were not very creative, either. The result of this produced a major chasm between mall management who answered to their real estate bosses and the stores and restaurants that operated in the mall.

When I started to represent malls, I also represented mall-based stores as clients so I was often seated on both sides of the table at once.

During my career, I had three different super-regional malls in three different geographic markets as clients in addition to the smaller boutique urban mall mentioned earlier. Each of these centers consisted of approximately 175 stores and all were the number one mall in their respective market area. Each mall had the usual collection of well-known chains in addition to local specialty stores and eateries.

The first of these centers that I represented was a suburban mall with an ice skating rink as one of its distinctive features. They had the dubious honor of being the home rink of the infamous figure skater Tonya Harding. However, fortunately for us, this was prior to her notorious crime. Back then, she was a just a good local skater and crowd pleaser for those watching her from the food court.

Our challenge was to create an institutional positioning campaign, funded by what is referred to as "lease required advertising."

In those days, many mall leases had a clause that required tenants to advertise in mall-sanctioned activities which were mall-directed and produced campaigns. The amount for each tenant varied according to their negotiated lease agreement, but usually calculated based on a percentage of a merchant's annual sales and/or the square footage of their footprint of their store or eatery in the mall.

Mall management would ante up a few bucks to support each tenant in this regard but the vast majority of the funds for the overall mall advertising effort came from these supplied tenant dollars.

An effective marketing campaign would have been possible to execute IF the merchants were willing participants, but unfortunately when I arrived at all of these malls, they were not. The problem and reason for their lack of their participation was due to the fact that they felt mall management was indifferent to their needs and stuck in a time warp which was demonstrated by offering them the same old win-lose advertising options year after year. Typical examples of this were tired old newspaper sections for mall-wide Sidewalk Sales or the annual mall Anniversary Sale or the boringly predictable holiday catalog that never represented the best stores or hottest merchandise available. The best stores did not want to participate because their image was at stake, and the image presented via these options were not in concert with their own company or corporate branding. There was also no real opportunity for them to promote their unique stores institutionally.

Most of the merchants would protest by not participating at all, and many of them would wait until the end of the year and negotiate a cash settlement. By the time that occurred, the damage was done; no effective marketing effort was achieved.

Of course, mall management took the tenant's money and put it straight to the developer's corporate bottom line and the merchants or the mall was never promoted the way it should have been done, consequently, sales were never what they could have been. I call this a "lose-lose" situation.

Whenever I get a new client or project, my first instinct is to look at the past to try to learn from previous behaviors both good and bad. It was nothing out of the ordinary for me to do so here.

Of course, when I first came on board at every mall I heard all about the lease required advertising issues from the marketing director. Once I had a basic overview of the current scenario, the first thing I would do is speak with the merchants directly. I wanted to hear their thoughts and opinions first-hand. I knew they were the critical component to any successful marketing effort we would design for the mall, and I felt it was imperative to show them that respect, especially since the majority of the budget to execute the advertising would come from them.

I would always hear the same stories and criticism. The mall would not listen to them and would not change with the times. The merchants wanted better options for their money and that was often broadcast—radio and TV. They also wanted to be treated fairly as the partners they were and with respect.

That is exactly what I delivered to them, and it started from day one by listening. By doing so, the merchants felt as if they were finally being heard, and our partnership was well-established from the beginning. This helped me to create win-win advertising strategies, presenting plans in concert with their individual store goals and the goals of the mall.

In one case, the first thing I did to demonstrate the change in execution was to create a major kick-off event. The plan was to announce the annual lease required advertising options to the merchants in a very creative and dynamic way to demonstrate that a new day had come. We threw a major party with all the bells and whistles—great food, cocktails and plenty of atmosphere. It was a themed event, a visual extravaganza that was accomplished with the help and support from many creative partners of mine to include my reps from all the TV and top radio stations in the market.

Everything about the event was fun and exciting thanks to Sherry, one of my partners, who excels at many things including creating special environments. She has a university degree in recreation so she was definitely capable and up to the task, but she stunned everyone with what she was able to pull off.

The whole strategy started with an audio invitation distributed to all the store managers or owners on tape. The party was held in one of the largest studios at one of the local TV stations on a Saturday night, instead of the usual pre-opening 8:00 a.m. coffee and donut affair that hardly anyone ever attended. The last thing any merchant wanted to do was to come in any earlier than necessary since their days were plenty long enough and usually a seven-day week of responsibility to boot.

The studio was transformed into a Camelot theme since the word Camelot could be transformed easily into the name of the mall and the elements of the story could be used perfectly as well. There was the large castle entry that attendees were greeted with upon arrival and as they passed through that portal, they found themselves in a world of tents encircling the room. These tents were hosted by my media partners, each orchestrating Camelotty-themed interactive games that were actually edutainment. Each game had a purpose in order to educate the merchants about the value of broadcast media, targeting, and the potential outcome of effective advertising. There were plenty of free gifts, gift certificates and merchandise handed out. Everyone left the games a winner.

The media representatives interacted with their potential customers in a non-sales environment. This helped lay a necessary foundation for these merchants, helping them to better understand the rationales for the newly devised annual plan, the elements of which were to be unveiled to them that night. It demonstrated the benefits of teamwork between the media, the mall, and me as their agent.

Establishing trust and communicating a rationale based on experience is essential to the success of any plan.

After they had cocktailed, eaten, and played games, we brought the annual lease required advertising plan to light via a large screen, professionally produced, and humorous video presentation. It started with testimonial-type video cuts from a selection of the store's well-known marketing leaders. We introduced our annual plan by showing these recognized retail leaders speaking about what they wanted to see going forward when it came to advertising with this mall. We then used footage from the *Camelot* movie—think roundtable—with new voiceover content explaining what was going to happen and served up packages and options for their lease required dollars for the upcoming year. It sent a very strong signal, supporting the total change of approach, and demonstrated a fresh creative spirit that would benefit all the participants. It also showed we were listening and put the people who helped guide our approach on screen for all to see and hear.

It was an incredibly successful kick-off event. Almost 80% of the stores' top management were in attendance, including the big box anchor tenants who rarely come to these types of meetings. Even more impressive was that this event occurred on a very nasty weather night in early January in the Pacific Northwest, which required extra effort to make the trek to the TV station downtown.

It helps to think and act like a retailer. I just did what retailers do and offered them a taste of their own behavior. We offered them a discount with a deadline to incent them to move quickly to sign up for their annual advertising commitment in full at the beginning of the year, instead of waiting. We offered them a sale in the form of a discount or credit to reduce their required lease obligation if they signed up within one week of the event.

Almost all of the merchants took advantage of our offer, and many did that night of the kick-off. This meant two things: I could negotiate media and creative on an annual basis which got us more bang and exposure than if we had done it piecemeal, and participation went from 10% to 90%. It continued like that for all the years we were involved with the mall. We gave them an offer they did not refuse and we executed an award-winning advertising campaign for the mall and the merchants alike. Of course, TV and radio advertising opportunities were offered in a variety of combinations, which they relished and ran toward.

Naturally, there was never enough money from any client I ever had to achieve what was possible, especially the malls. I usually made up the shortfall to deliver what I wanted to do, always with the help of my fantastic media partners. By treating them as partners, and sharing with them all the information necessary to include the budget I had to work with, my reps gave me lots of value-added extras in the way of free promotional support on-air and off. They knew they would get the truth from me and get a fair shake and share of that budget. They always knew where they stood with me and why. The media gave my clients many gifts with purchase in exchange for a relationship they could count on.

Loyalty to those who deserve it and honesty are the most important aspects of business relationships.

The lease required ad campaign executed for this first mall we represented became the template for all three I eventually had as clients. This was a combination of testimonial radio and TV spots using real customers of the stores. Yes, we still offered the holiday catalog, redesigned of course, because there were still some merchants who wanted it in the mix.

For two of the malls I also offered a jewel of an idea in the annual offerings—an opportunity to be in a complete promotional extravaganza served up as a 30-minute TV show, a sitcom about shopping, that was actually and technically an infomercial called "a day at the mall."©

This concept was created and directed by me with the help of my long-time co-pilot Walt, one of the most talented directors around, and Jeff, a great cameraman from one of the local TV stations. Together we created several episodes for each mall, each one centered on a different category of merchandise—clothing for the back to school show, home goods for another. The shows were shot reality-style, in the mall, during normal business hours. The action took place in the stores that signed up to be in the shows and we developed the storyline for each store around the merchandise they wanted to feature. For example, a kitchenware store wanted to show pasta makers so the story in that case was about planning a dinner party and wanting to serve something different than usual. Homemade pasta was the answer.

The cast was a group of terrific experienced local actors and since my best friend Sam had now become the best local broadcast talent agent she recommended and delivered the perfect characters for the show that included a middle-aged mom, her teenage daughter, her senior father and her controlling best girlfriend. There was a young 30-something couple, a 40-ish self-proclaimed shop-o-holic career woman, and a typical and loveable shopping-clueless 20-year-old young man.

The content evolved organically as the stores signed up. The actors were directed with a basic storyline for each segment. Since I knew all about shopping neurosis first-hand, I knew what the storylines should be. The actors were selected based on their real-life feelings about shopping, and the shows came together in the editing process by selecting the best non-scripted bits. We inserted soliloquies into the shows to give background on each personality type and to enable our characters to present how they felt about what they were doing, to establish the motivations of each character in the plot. The personnel of the participating stores were also on camera, playing themselves. In the end, every store was thrilled with their piece of the action.

I even created commercial breaks in the shows, selling spots to some of the retailers in the mall who were TV advertising regulars, to give the show's format authenticity. It was also listed in *TV Guide* as a legitimate program offering, rather than the 30-minute infomercial it really was.

All bases were covered when it came to publicity for the shows, too. The local daily newspaper editor, a former network TV news director who was well-known and who wrote an on-going media column, proclaimed in his column after seeing an advance of one of the shows that one should "look for a day at the mall© to have a longer run than most sitcoms." The ratings for each episode beat most of the competition running against it and that included some very well-known established shows during the very important time slot called "prime access" between 6:30 and 8:00 p.m. when each episode ran. They also rebroadcasted the episodes in late night so they received maximum exposure.

The shows were smart and entertaining and great local press increased the viewership and results. Most importantly, the concept totally connected with our primary target, the chief shopper, in a very humorous and relatable way.

I was very pleased that "a day at the mall©" not only won an international marketing award after my client Michelle, one of the mall's marketing directors, entered the campaign into that competition but most important to me was that it was a major success for the retailers who took part. The show concept was also used as the basis for an ongoing TV commercial series to promote the malls institutionally, promoting special events, and to sell gift certificates for every occasion from Mother's Day to Christmas.

So all around and for many reasons, my baby was a hit with the right people. I was never motivated by awards, but results. In all our efforts to bring change to the malls we represented, we were supported by several forward-thinking mall marketing directors who were excited and benefited by the happier retail climate we created.

As it turned out, "a day at the mall©" was a major gift that kept on giving including the partnership with Rebecca, our first mall marketing director client who later joined our company. She was an instrumental partner in growing our mall client base.

I could not be more proud of anything I ever did in my agency days. It was proof positive that when you do what you love, play to your strengths, partner with the best people, and create win-win propositions, good things happen.

20

FREE ADVICE

In Conclusion

To sum up my experiences in the world of marketing is to acknowledge that some things never change.

Regardless of whether it is in the mailbox or inbox, TV or livestream, radio or podcast, or the written word on newsprint, glossy stock or on a screen or billboard, the basic principles of marketing have never changed.

You can call it branding or image building, but a product or service business must convey a consistency in personality and deliverables in order to keep and build an audience and customer base. An entity must also grow and change if the times demand it, but in most cases, successful businesses are built on a long-lasting foundation and identity.

I reread a great book from my marketing library recently called *Success.* There are many great minds represented in its pages and one relevant thought for marketing success is appropriate to quote here:

"Taking a risk is a creative act. It may mean approaching a task or situation in a completely different way."

I could not agree more because there are no certainties in any marketing effort and one should start there when advising others.

Advertising works, but bad advertising can destroy any company. "Junk mail" is not a term of endearment or coined by marketers. Who likes being asked to donate to a charity while checking out at the grocery store? No one I have spoken with, and I have done more than enough research on these types of tactics to know how the chief shopper thinks.

Technology has made it easier to avoid some advertising efforts, however, there are awards for the best TV and radio commercials and printed materials—creative efforts in all mediums. These campaigns are noticed and talked about in popular culture. It is always good to remember that there would be no entertainment industry without advertising revenue, and that includes professional sports. Football and basketball heroes, the Olympic stars, and all the rest of these amazing athletes are known beyond their hometowns because of the exposure in broad based media. These spokespeople are used to sell products because they are household names as a result.

I think the internet can be an excellent platform for the right occasions. It is an easy access library and research tool, and many think it's a great place to meet Prince or Princess Charming. Others use it for connecting with old friends or networking with business acquaintances. We have also seen that it can spark a revolution, provide a convenient political soapbox, and it can help elect a president. Media—old or new—is powerful and should be used wisely and for specific reasons to achieve the best results.

Shopping online has had little impact on overall retail spending or profits for many, but there are always exceptions. The JC Penney catalog did $4 billion in sales at its peak, and when they moved it onto the web, it produced $1.5 billion. Women still love to get catalogs.

Contrary to what some people think, malls are not dead. The number of malls exploded in recent times, from 300 to now over 1200 entities in 2017. This growth of retail outlets happened in a relatively short period of years. Naturally, consolidation is now occurring. However, mall occupancy rates are also very high now at 93%. Even Amazon is opening and acquiring brick and mortar stores in several retail sectors.

I learned long ago that "had what I wanted," not cost or convenience, is the primary purchase motivator.

Retail is still all about experience and best delivered when all the senses are stimulated. If I, as a chief shopper, only bought what I set out to purchase, I would have more money in the bank and have bought much less.

The best purchases are often surprises, and often acquired because of someone else's encouragement, live and in person. Shopping is a social activity, often referred to as retail therapy for a reason. Effective therapy is not done solo.

The fact is that people don't always shop to buy something specific; they shop for entertainment and to connect with others, and when in the right mood, and in the right setting, they buy more. That is why brick and mortar retailers spend so much energy and resources creating the right environment with music playing and all the rest of the hullabaloo. Starbucks was founded on the principle of duplicating the cafes in Europe where people come to hang out and be together and this company is well-known for being a place people like to frequent. Their success is proof of that fundamental belief I hold dear.

Most importantly, salespeople affect any sale more than ANY other factor. For this reason alone, if there is no sales force involved, maximum sales will not be realized regardless of the product or service. No salespeople equals less sales. Customer service is still needed and wanted. Walmart is still on top and now takes orders online with in-store pickup. Walmart is also giving discounts to purchases picked up in-store; they're no fools. Target now dedicates lots of their floor space to food for good reason because they, too, want shoppers to come into their stores. They know they will increase sales overall as a result. Amazon knows that, too, when it comes to food; like so many other products, stores matter.

I visited a Dairy Queen recently and I asked if their special "$5 buck" deal was still in effect, and the answer was, "Yes, unfortunately." Apparently, their TV promotion was working, but I also thought they should do a better job communicating to their employees what this promotion meant to their bottom line. This would also help their employees better deliver good customer service with a smile.

Females buy 80% of all goods and services and may affect the rest of the purchasing with a strong opinion, but that does not mean they pay for everything. Women are definitely the chief shoppers even if someone tells you otherwise. Minivans are a great example of understanding who holds the purse and makes the decisions. Smart automakers knew this long ago.

Recently according to *The New York Times* in a front page story, "after 40 years of catering to younger customers, advertisers and media executives are coming to a different realization: older people aren't so bad after all." Companies are again focused on "those 55 and up who have been largely ignored in most of their media plans until recently." I never ignored this market, I always played to it. Some of us always knew this chief shopper demographic. The number one lesson in advertising is: Know your target and most often, with few exceptions, the number one target is the "chief shopper," a woman over 40.

Retail workers also significantly affect retail sales in many ways. A company's own employees are often their best and consistent customers, and their paychecks are like boomerangs going back into the coffers of the stores in which they work. I know this from my own history working in the department store. Androids can't do this, and this is another reason why retailing suffers without the personal touch. Never ignore a client's workforce when it comes to marketing. Their wallets matter and so do their opinions. They should be proud of their company image because they are the best brand ambassadors.

Great advertising is all about standing out. It is hard to

stand out online. When you don't stand out it is often due to "clutter." All media tries to minimize this issue. Positioning is part of the plan; the best position is one with fewer or, better still, no other distractions. TV advertising became more challenging with the birth of hundreds of cable channels. There are so many choices and now there is on demand viewing as well. However, to this day, in my opinion, TV is still the enduring technology for advertisers. Just ask Apple; one TV spot with memorable creative can cause a sensation and create a furor and massive demand for a new product.

Billboards work well for this reason, too, because if selected properly, a company can get maximum attention with less clutter and competition. However, creative can make or break the best location, too.

Less is more, so keep your message simple.

Radio, once dubbed "theatre of the mind," has its own strength in the mix and can be very effective if used with dynamic creative execution and selective placement. I was always happy to pay a premium for a very narrow time frame for my commercials to air in order to reach the greatest number of listeners.

The best way to distribute coupons is directly to the chief shopper. It is well recognized that 80% of sales often comes from 20% of customers. Very few businesses are prepared or capable of selling globally. Most customers live within five miles of a business they frequent.

Most people are followers, not leaders, and so it is advised to watch who you are following so you don't become a lemming. This reminds me of my dry cleaners who have a Facebook page, as most businesses do. Why do dry cleaners need a Facebook page? In this case it was because their grandkids told them it was a good idea. Of course, their grandkids are not their primary target market and the grandparents are not marketing experts either.

A company's website is often their yellow page ad, coupon book, catalog and medium of choice. It is used to deliver video content. It is often a company's front desk and its salesforce too. It is almost everything marketing rolled into one. "If life were only like this," said Woody Allen in *Annie Hall*.

Again, marketing is best delivered by pro-fessionals, and a simple message is best. Too many options and too many choices and too much copy becomes wallpaper fast. It is imperative to know what business you are in and strive to perfect that craft, instead of becoming a jack of all trades, master of none. Talent shows what you can do; artistry shows who you are.

Recently I heard a discussion on PBS radio about internet security that got my attention. The interviewer was asking a woman what she knew about the safety of her identity online. This woman explained that she was a college graduate and in my opinion, from what I heard, she did not come off as a fool but she was shocked to hear that her identity was at risk. Even though she had heard all the chatter about it, and knew the pitfalls of sharing, she thought she had avoided any problems since she had been "careful." She was told of the many hackers and their abilities and ultimately, every move she made was being noticed and tracked by advertisers, regardless of whether she was careful or not.

After the interview, and after hearing from the legal experts on this broadcast, when asked what she thought now she said she "thought it was creepy." When I hear a chief shopper describe something as "creepy" I take notice. Being a good listener and exposing yourself to many different people and opinions helps to develop strategic and successful marketing outcomes.

I also heard a report on "60 Minutes" recently when an expert in internet technology said the results of too much technology on humans was referred to in his industry as "brain hacking." This is what the experts call it. It will be interesting to see where this goes, however good marketers should try their best to contribute to a healthy and positive atmosphere because good behavior will pay off in the end.

Thanks to social media, smart phones, and tons of data, companies can track customers by purchase history, search history, postings, and so much more.

Currently, one can be analyzed geographically, psychographically, financially and almost every way but physically. The obsessive following of one's every shopping move, trying to anticipate needs, hounding customers to death with too many offers and reminders is not good marketing. Spam filters were invented to stop this just like answering machines, caller ID, and no-call lists were invented to stop overzealous and unwanted telemarketing calls.

Good marketers are not hound dogs.

Marketing is still about targeting and then building a case for purchase with that group. Most important is to have what your customers want; you can find that out by interacting with them on a regular basis. It is advised to be careful who and what you ask always focusing on the chief shopper.

Marketing is still about great branding that endures. There is no reason to fix what is not broken. Great branding works worldwide because great is great everywhere.

Marketing is still about teamwork. It takes a village to deliver a successful ad campaign because no one can do everything well. It takes dedication and years of experience to become an expert. A CEO, president, vice president of operations, or even a vice president of marketing needs creative partners and counsel in order to execute effective advertising for their organization. Operating as a dictator in any of these posts is dangerous. You definitely don't get the best partners by behaving like this. Clients are best served when they recognize their role in the process, and as the old saying goes: Companies get the advertising they deserve.

Marketing success still depends on the philosophy that filters throughout an organization starting from the top. Respect is the key word for the greater team, inside an organization and out. Recognition that because one is good at one aspect of business or marketing does not mean one is good at everything.

Interpersonal skills, also known as people skills, matter most to be a successful marketer. There is a difference between social networking and social skills. The ability to problem solve, in addition to excellent listening, leadership, written and oral communication abilities, not necessarily in that order, are essential for success. It's important to always remember that trust comes from honesty.

Nothing fundamental has changed since I began my career in retail or marketing. It still takes heart, smarts, and guts.

I respectfully rest my case.

ACKNOWLEDGMENTS

There are hundreds of people to thank who enabled me to deliver the many stories shared in this book, in addition to the many other client campaigns executed over the years. This includes all of my media and creative partners who taught me the marketing business in real time and all of my clients who trusted me with their businesses.

A special shout-out to my two agency partners, Deidre Mosher and Susan Goschie, who supported me and helped craft our company reputation for creative excellence and outstanding client service.

A toast to our agency staff and consultants who always delivered no matter the deadline or the challenge: Sharon Betzing, Janey Biossat, Fred Black, Julie Chase, Tori Brock Gandy, Linda Daniels, Deb Diers, Janet Farrington, Gayle Goschie, Cheryl Grant, Sharon Hanson, Julie Jelline, Renee Kuhn, Susie McAbee, Enid Neilsen, Suzan Nolan, Elaine Opsitnik, and Rebecca Sonniksen.

To those in the media who showed extraordinary loyalty and made special contributions, I am very grateful to: Aby Briton, Janis Miller Chittick, Jim Cummings, Dusty Davidson, Elaine Durst, Maureen Fisher, Karen Hansen, Kate Ivory, Teddi Jones, Jack Kliger, David Lockhert, Connie Martin, Gwen Mason, Jole McMurdie, Jade Metcalf, Sandy Nigro, Lois Petrik, Lorraine Robertson, Patty Rouas, Mick Schafbaugh, Jamie Sexton, Bob Torheim, Maggi White, and Aki Yokoyama.

To the significant contributors to our agency creative efforts: Michael Bard, Dale Champlin, Jon Deshler, Walt Dimick, Sam Downey, Jeff Gustin, Marcelle Kauffman, Rhonda Kennedy, Lance Limbocker, Sherry May, Jon Newton, Gary Nolton, Vana O'Brien, Mike Quinn, Ron Rinella, David Smith, Jeffrey Smith, Nannette Troutman, Wendy Westerwelle, Patty Williams, and Michael Wolfgang.

To the clients who allowed me the opportunity to shine: Kelly Alston, Tom Atiyeh, John Barker, Stan Blauer, Bill Boston, Janet Day, Rodney Dickenson, Michelle Driano, Jon Enyart, Bill Failing, Mitch Greenlick, Arlee Jensen, Berna Kieler, Eric Kieler, Soren Kieler, Michael Luce, Lou Menashe, Deryk Marian, Michael Moises, Anne Naito-Campbell, Sam Naito, Elmer Nofziger, Don Rasmussen, Harry Roberts, Jean Rosenbaum, Ariel Rubenstein, Paul Schlesinger, Ralph Schlesinger, Carl Schumacher, Mark Schumacher, Joseph Treves, and Doug Worsley.

A special salute to Steve Mosher and Herman Goschie who offered special business advice and support when it was needed.

www.ingramcontent.com/pod-product-compliance
Lightning Source LLC
Chambersburg PA
CBHW070819100426
42813CB00033B/3434/J

* 9 7 8 0 9 9 8 1 2 0 8 6 7 *